The Rehearsal

The Rehearsal

By JEAN ANOUILH

TRANSLATED BY PAMELA HANSFORD JOHNSON
AND KITTY BLACK

COWARD-McCANN, Inc.
NEW YORK

*Copyright © 1961 by Jean Anouilh,
Pamela Hansford Johnson, and Kitty Black*

All rights reserved. This book, or parts thereof, may not be reproduced in any form without permission in writing from the Publisher.

THE REHEARSAL is the sole property of the authors and is fully protected by copyright. It may not be acted by professionals or by amateurs without written consent. Public readings and radio or television broadcasts are likewise forbidden. All inquiries concerning rights should be addressed to the author's agent, Dr. Jan van Loewen, International Copyright Agency, 81-83 Shaftesbury Avenue, London W.1.

PHOTO CREDIT: FRIEDMAN—ABELES

MANUFACTURED IN THE UNITED STATES OF AMERICA

The Rehearsal

Characters

THE COUNT
THE COUNTESS, *his wife*
HORTENSIA, *his mistress*
HERO, *his friend*
VILLEBOSSE, *his wife's lover*
MONSIEUR DAMIENS, *the Countess's lawyer*
LUCILE, *Monsieur Damiens' goddaughter*

The action takes place in the château of Ferbroques. The characters wear eighteenth-century costume.

Act One

SCENE ONE

A *salon. The* COUNTESS *and* MONSIEUR DAMIENS *enter, in Louis XIV costumes.*

COUNTESS. Monsieur Damiens, I must thank you most sincerely for lending us your goddaughter.

M. DAMIENS. To oblige you, madame, is the first and most pleasant of my duties. You had need of her, so it was most natural that she should come to Ferbroques.

COUNTESS. What would have become of us without her? My poor aunt, the late Marquise, was the most whimsical creature alive. The idea of leaving us Ferbroques on condition that we spent a month here every spring, was touching enough. Ferbroques is a desert; she herself could never endure more than a week here. She spent the whole winter in Paris sighing after Ferbroques, but as soon as the fine weather came, she hurried off elsewhere. It is only fair to say the poor woman was at the mercy of several eminent doctors. Although she enjoyed excellent health, the summer was hardly long enough for her to take all her cures. When she'd drunk all her waters, taken mud baths in all the four corners of Europe, she was left with hardly enough time to return to Paris and order her dresses, swearing by all she held dear—ourselves, I have no doubt—that next spring she would come and live in her château. But when spring came round again, her doctors sent her off to quaff new health from new springs. Death delivering her from miraculous cures, she laid it on us to implement her vows.

M. DAMIENS. A sensitive thought . . .

COUNTESS. Yes. A month in the country, providing you give a ball or two, passes quickly enough. And how could we reject Ferbroques? It is a jewel. But the clause in the will, enjoining us to bring up twelve orphan children in the west wing, must have given her great satisfaction when she wrote it.

M. DAMIENS. Perhaps a concern for Christian charity . . . ?

COUNTESS. My aunt was a child of the Enlightenment. It could only have been sheer politeness which, on her deathbed, dictated this small gesture toward heaven. She detested children. She had a wretched drudge of a footman—poor Jules, he died two months after she did, worn out by peace and quiet—whose special task it was to precede her in public places and clear all children from her path. It was a phobia with her, ever since she was hit on the head by a diabolo in a garden.

M. DAMIENS. Perhaps a touch of remorse . . . ?

COUNTESS. Monsieur Damiens, you did not know my aunt. She was an extraordinary woman, incapable of remorse of any kind. . . . No, for my own part, I can only see one explanation for the founding of this orphanage: the desire to play a delicious posthumous trick on the Count and myself. Tiger, of course, took it extremely well. He adored arguing with my aunt. "Splendid!" he cried, when the lawyer had finished. "She wants twelve scamps to deafen us one month in the year? We'll parry the thrust, my dear: we'll seek out twelve little deaf-mutes." I'm perfectly certain that when she heard his riposte, my aunt must have turned in her family mausoleum at Passy. Particularly since, after her long battle with Tiger, this meant that he had scored the final point. Short of rising up in her shroud to haunt him—and the poor dear had far too much good taste to stoop to anything of that sort—there was nothing she could do to him ever again.

M. DAMIENS. Yet you gave up your project? I thought I heard children playing when I came through the park?

COUNTESS. Yes. Unfortunately, the will specified "orphans," and although the world is brimming over with misery, when it comes to laying your hands on twelve orphaned deaf-mutes, you find it's extremely difficult. We had all sorts offered us—lame ones, blind ones, deaf-mutes with the full complement of parents, or orphans speaking as well as you or I. We might, perhaps, have assembled an assortment in the course of time, but Tiger, who has never had the courage to pursue his revenges very far, decided, after thinking it over, that it might all prove a little sad. We collected twelve orphans fully equipped with vocal cords, and took refuge in the east wing. Ferbroques is enormous, thank God. The only problem was to organize the grand charity ball Tiger and I decided to give for the opening of the orphanage. Tiger is quite marvelous at such things.

One of the last men of our time to realize that futility must be taken quite seriously. In the course of a single night he conceived the theme of the ball, the theme of the whole entertainment. I can't tell you what it is, because it's still a great secret. Next morning, the decorators arrived from Paris. We've had a delicious week of hammering and high fever, gripping the nails in our teeth, matching patterns in the middle of the night, living on crusts of bread handed up to us on our ladders, where we perched like cockatoos. Tiger was wonderful. He had a new idea every minute. He killed two decorators under him—they had to be put to bed exhausted in the gatehouse. In short, all was going well, the great day was approaching and then one morning—disaster! The orphans arrived. We had forgotten all about them. That was when I sent you my telegram, and you were kind enough to lend us your goddaughter to help us out. I hope she's happy here?

M. DAMIENS. She adores children.

COUNTESS. It is, I believe, her profession?

M. DAMIENS. Yes. When her mother died, she had to find a situation. She drifted into kinderculture.

COUNTESS. What— Oh well, I suppose one culture is much like another. I prefer my roses; they don't grizzle and squawk. Have you ever seen the Ferbroques greenhouses? I have never seen so many marvels gathered together.

M. DAMIENS. I have seen nothing. Since I arrived last night, I have only had time to fit my costume and try to learn my part.

COUNTESS. It was so kind of you to help us out at the last minute. The unexpected defection of Gontaut-Biron, who should have played Trivelin, had thrown Tiger into the depths of despair. I feared the worst.

M. DAMIENS. Indeed?

COUNTESS. Indeed. Tiger has the most unexpected capacity for setting store on things. Apparently he behaved marvelously in '40, fighting on alone on the Loire when everyone else had gone off to Toulouse. He had a little cannon, more or less tied together with string, which couldn't be brought to bear properly. He held out with it against a cloud of Pomeranian grenadiers. Five hours after the armistice, he was still blazing away, though the others were waving white flags at him and shouting through their loudspeakers that he was making himself ridiculous. The fact that France had surrendered didn't bother him in the least. But when he'd fired his last shell, he asked the Germans for a bath; shaved himself, had a manicure—his orderly, the only other survivor, was a manicurist—and never mentioned the defeat again. But a ball in jeopardy!—that's different. He'd be quite capable of killing himself, like Vatel at Chantilly.

M. DAMIENS. I'm honored to think that by taking this tiny part I can spare him so painful an obligation. At twenty I had quite a little reputation as an amateur.

COUNTESS. I'm sure you still have. A lawyer never really stops playing in comedy—in tragedy too, alas, sometimes. Before the war, you had to go to the Odéon to find a more fustian performance than an attorney general demanding the death sentence.

COUNT. (*The* COUNT *enters, also in costume*) Well, do we rehearse? The play is by Marivaux. We can't make it up as we go along. Where is your goddaughter, Monsieur

Damiens? It's quite outrageous for those twelve orphans to monopolize her. We need her too, you know.

M. DAMIENS. She was putting them to bed, and then coming to join us.

COUNT. Be a good soul. Go and snatch her from the claws of those twelve little horrors. We cannot begin without her.

> MONSIEUR DAMIENS *goes out. The* COUNT *sits down near the* COUNTESS.

My dear, we've made a splendid start. To perform the play during dinner was a ravishing idea. One character gets up from table and calls to another; they start to talk, and everyone listens, thinking they've really got something to say. The general flavor will be rather startling at first, but I, at my end of the table, and you, at yours, shall have taken care right from the beginning of the meal to give the conversation a slight touch of the eighteenth century—to make the transition imperceptible. As soon as the dialogue seems in danger of dragging, another character enters, a servant, who draws them aside. Everyone is stupefied. What badly behaved servants we have! Then they recognize the play. Ah, but it's too late now—it has begun. We have bypassed the moment of terror which seizes sophisticated persons when they find themselves seated before a stage full of amateurs.

COUNTESS. There's only one snag. The play is by Marivaux. Most of them won't have read it.

COUNT. All the better. They'll think I wrote it myself. Besides, you mustn't be hard on them. They're not very bright, of course. But no one expects people of our class to produce geniuses—we're not numerically strong enough to afford such luxuries. We leave that to the crowd, which pours out a million plowboys so that once in three or four generations they can triumphantly throw up a gold medalist or a President of the Republic. All we ask of our own kind is cohesion and continuity. For several centuries we've all shown a talent in that direction. We do our best.

COUNTESS. Another snag. If they listen to the play, the food will get cold.

COUNT. That can't be helped. We always feed them too well —it will make a change. You are certainly seeing the dark side tonight, my dear. . . . Besides, the supper menu can be compiled to fit the dramatic situations. I'll bring on the lobster and champagne the moment the interest flags; nothing but toothpicks in the lyrical moments to make them go through the motions of meditation. One has to help such people. They may be frivolous, but they are not devoid of talent. Nothing makes a man more thoughtful than trying to dislodge a shred of meat from between two molars. If they go through the motions, they may even arrive at a thought—by association of ideas. After all, they weren't any more stupid in the Grand Siècle, when they really did appreciate good writers. I think this child will be charming as Silvia.

COUNTESS. I think she lacks sparkle. I wonder why you turned everything upside down to give her the part.

COUNT. That's just it! She'll be a splendid contrast to your dazzling friends. She burns with an inward fire which she cloaks under a veil of shyness. It will make a change from all those professional beauties who set fire to any wood in order to make a blaze. They burn with an entrancing flame all the evening, and then, when you've gone home with them, the fire's dead out. Besides, nobody knows her. And for these people who call everyone by nicknames, it'll be an additional piquancy not to have the slightest idea who she is.

COUNTESS. You wouldn't, by any chance, be in love with her?

COUNT. I? Not in the least.

COUNTESS. I'm relieved to hear it.

COUNT. The drawback is this Louis Quatorze costume and the wig. It makes one look like a spaniel. But—and it must be part of my aunt's revenge—Ferbroques is an eighteenth-century château and we couldn't avoid it. In a Renaissance manor house, like your Grandlieu, we might have created something extraordinary. I would have produced a little play by Marguerite de Navarre which is adorable and which none of them could have known.

COUNTESS. In any case, it's too late for that now.

COUNT. Of course it's too late. But I shan't sleep until I've thought of something to make this costume amusing. Of course, we might put all the men into beards, or play the whole thing in trousers and top hats, but that's a cheap way of being original, and they'd never understand the joke. One mustn't overestimate the intelligence of one's audience.

COUNTESS. How old is she?

COUNT. Just twenty. You must help me think.

COUNTESS. About what?

COUNT. The Louis Quatorze costumes. We could very well drown in banality on their account. What a hideous thought!

He takes off his wig and fans himself with it.

COUNTESS. Supposing we told everyone not to wear their wigs?

COUNT. (*Looking at himself in a mirror*) Of course it's much better. Particularly because the child has hair of a really exceptional color—it would be a crime to powder it.

COUNTESS. I find her rather ugly.

COUNT. So do I. I was speaking of the color of her hair.

COUNTESS. You know you're quite free, Tiger. Do me the justice to admit that I have never meddled with your love affairs. Don't play the fool too much with her, all the same. Damiens has been my family solicitor for more than thirty years, and I shouldn't like him to have anything to hold against us.

COUNT. What do you take me for, my dear? I have grave faults, I know, but no one has ever questioned my good manners. In fact, my manner, my coat of arms and my name are more or less all I can call my own . . . if I except this château and the dozen orphans.

COUNTESS. That's no obstacle.

COUNT. I beg your pardon! It's an obstacle to a great deal. My father, who was a most perfect man, before he died took great care to put me on guard against that very thing. Though I was very young, I have never forgotten it—the only advice he ever thought it necessary to give me. It was a few hours before his death. The Bishop and his entire clergy were waiting in the anteroom to administer extreme unction; my father asked them to send me in first. "My boy," he said to me, "I have realized rather belatedly that I have never paid much attention to you. I have very little time. I'm packing my traps and Monseigneur is waiting to hear what I have to declare. So far as the family honor is concerned, I know I can trust you. As for the rest, you can rely on your instincts—it has no great importance anyway. There is just one thing. You're young; you'll want to enjoy yourself. Always follow your own desires, but with women of your own world. With any others, it always turns out badly. You end by marrying a housemaid or an opera singer and get yourself ostracized, or you father bastards on some little dressmaker and when they grow up they turn against you and foment revolutions. . . . Peccadilloes, if you like, my boy, none of us are angels—but in your own world. Now send in the Bishop. I must empty my bag before him and let him give me official clearance . . . the time has come."

A short pause. Suddenly he says:
An admirable man, my father. I never got to know him, but I realized then that I loved him with my whole heart.

COUNTESS. (*After another silence*) I have the impression, Tiger—believe me, this isn't a reproach—that you really did give him your whole heart and have never given away more than a fragment of it since.

COUNT. (*Shaking himself*) My dear, how depressing your conversation is today! We're making ourselves absurd—this is melodrama. Besides, you know I'm extremely fond of you. I've never had such a feeling for anyone else. But don't tell Hortensia, or I shall be involved in quite another drama.

COUNTESS. Do you tell all your mistresses that you love them?

COUNT. One has to. Women are such sticklers for etiquette. I really believe you're the only woman to whom I have never said it.

COUNTESS. What a singular compliment! Do you expect me to thank you? Because it was never true.

COUNT. Because there is something quite different between us, something delicate and charming, which releases me from the obligation of lying to you. We really must take a grip on ourselves, Eliane! Or we shall become maudlin in a moment. Love is the daily bread of the poor; we cannot allow ourselves, at this late date, to sit down under our family portraits and cry our eyes out because we have never known what love is. There are a thousand things in the world more important than a shattering disturbance of that sort. It's like the bottle you drain in a single evening for the sake of a flourish: you pay for two hours' excitement with an interminable night of headaches and vomiting. The price is too high. I have no ambition whatsoever, except to turn my life into a successful entertainment; which is very much more difficult, let me tell you, than boring everyone by beating your breast and suffering. Besides . . . I don't want to be indiscreet, my dear, but if you want to play at that little game, you've always got Villebosse—Villebosse or another, what do I care? The world is full of ranters and roarers.

COUNTESS. Villebosse bores me.

COUNT. I find him delightful. He's young and handsome. He is always ready to dive off the highest board, or jump through a circle of fire at the slightest provocation. You don't really expect me to sing the praises of that fellow, do you?

COUNTESS. Be polite, Tiger. That fellow is my lover.

COUNT. *(Suddenly a little dry)* That's enough, Eliane. We're on the verge of becoming disgusting. I don't like some conversations. My ideas may be liberal but my words are narrow. You are free. I am free. We like each other very much, but we're here to give an entertainment, which is a real gamble in this wilderness, as you very well know. There are some things infinitely more important, I beg you to believe, than our little private emotions. People are never bored at our parties. With a single folly we could destroy the reputation of fifteen years in one evening.

He looks at himself in the mirror.

Do you really think it's better without the wig? Yes, there's no doubt about it, you're absolutely right. There's a certain incompleteness, which makes the Louis Quatorze more endearing. I'll rush off instructions to everyone not to wear their wigs. *(He kisses her hand)* You are always right. I'm devoted to you, Eliane.

He goes out. HORTENSIA *enters by another door. She is also in costume.*

HORTENSIA. Oh, I'm sorry! They told me Tiger was with you.

COUNTESS. He's just gone out.

HORTENSIA. He thinks of nothing but this ball. We never see him nowadays.

COUNTESS. My dear Hortensia, I'm well past the time when I loved Tiger enough to be jealous of his parties.

HORTENSIA. Oh, I'm not suffering unduly! Are we going to rehearse? I don't feel very sure of myself.

COUNTESS. That's the first time I've heard you say that.

HORTENSIA. Acting in a comedy isn't exactly my métier.

COUNTESS. Maybe that's because the text isn't your own invention—for once. We're waiting for the child who is playing Silvia.

HORTENSIA. Why on earth did Tiger insist on giving her the part?

COUNTESS. She's charming.

HORTENSIA. I think she lacks sparkle.

COUNTESS. You're quite wrong. She burns with a hidden fire that she cloaks under a veil of shyness. She isn't like those dazzling young women who use any sort of wood to make a blaze. They burn with an entrancing flame all the evening, and then, it seems, when you've gone home with them, the fire's dead out.

HORTENSIA. What is this new caprice of Tiger's, making her act with us? Of course, he's given a part to his valet as well, but I hope that once the play's over, he'll send her back to the kitchen with him.

COUNTESS. Let me disillusion you again. From what I know of Tiger, providing she has had a little success in the play, he'll dance with her the entire evening.

HORTENSIA. That would be most disagreeable. Until now, your house was one of the very rare places where one could be sure of meeting only one's friends.

COUNTESS. My dear, through fifteen years of care and ceaseless vigilance, Tiger has taken the trouble to become the unchallenged arbiter of everything accounted good taste in Paris. If he had only spent half the same energy in business, he would be fabulously rich. Now, he can allow himself the luxury of doing as he pleases. He refuses to meet his broker socially, but if he has decided that the goddaughter of my family solicitor can be received, received she will be.

HORTENSIA. It's grotesque! Isn't she some sort of nursemaid here?

COUNTESS. If these children were our own, I doubt if Tiger would have dared. She is here to supervise the orphans left us in my aunt's will. All twelve of them. Tiger has a genius for taking advantage of nuances. Besides—I'd rather not hide it from you—I believe he was dying to have her.

HORTENSIA. There is a certain bitterness in your remarks, Eliane.

COUNTESS. Far be it from me to stoop to bitterness, my dear —or to spite. Your liaison with Tiger is entirely agreeable to me. Since we are both at liberty to do as we please, it pleases me to admit that you're exactly the right person for him. He is very much in love with you, you know.

HORTENSIA. Is that true?

COUNTESS. So he says. It remains to be seen whether everything Tiger says is true. I gave up verifying his statements a long time ago.

HORTENSIA. At all events, I give you my word he won't dance the night through with her.

COUNTESS. But no scenes! That would be the best way of making up his mind for him.

HORTENSIA. Thank you for your good advice, Eliane, but I know Tiger fairly well myself.

COUNTESS. Your dress is utterly delightful!

HORTENSIA. Yours suits you to perfection!

COUNTESS. I can't tell you how grateful I am to you for being beautiful! I should have been horribly mortified if Tiger had taken up with a mere nobody. Turn around! How amusingly Jacquot has interpreted the paniers! He really is a genius. One may be lured away for a season—one always comes back to him in the end.

HORTENSIA. Léonor still makes your clothes, doesn't she? It's quite staggering how she's managed to produce a real Louis Quatorze in spite of using the little side drape that only came out this season. Will she be there?

COUNTESS. Who?

HORTENSIA. (*A little spitefully*) Léonor. Of course she's coming. That woman goes everywhere—even to Tiger's parties!

COUNTESS. Particularly to Tiger's parties.

HORTENSIA. Why particularly? Everyone knows that Léonor, who started out as a milliner's apprentice, has had a tremendous social success. He's merely swimming with the tide.

COUNTESS. Tiger never swims with a tide he hasn't created himself. We must do him that justice. I'm sure that if there hadn't been a certain personal interest mixed up in it, he would have become very punctilious all of a sudden on the subject of Léonor. He's the most easygoing man in the world, but he maintains that if you want to play a game, you should play it really well. Quite happy he may be, drinking beer in bars with taxi drivers, but he only opens his house to people of his own world.

HORTENSIA. What on earth has given that woman the extraordinary entree everywhere? The fact that she's a genius?

COUNTESS. Tiger doesn't rate genius as a social asset. My dear, he is merely exercising hs royal prerogative. He feels sure enough of himself to ennoble whom he pleases. He invites her into his house because he wants her, and because she said no to him four years ago.

HORTENSIA. How sweet of you to tell me!

COUNTESS. I'm telling you because it's all old history. But to to have resisted Tiger—which is a pretty rare distinction, my dear—is quite enough to get one received everywhere.

HORTENSIA. Eliane, you're wasting your barbs. Tiger or anybody else, I am quite determined never to suffer.

COUNTESS. That's precisely why I believe he is so very attached to you. And so am I. *(She kisses her)* Dear little Hortensia! After all, one has so few friends.

HERO *enters, carrying his wig.*

Ah! Here is Hero! Hero, I love you very much.

HERO. You took the words out of my mouth, Eliane. Do we rehearse? Tiger is a tyrant, making us put on our costumes three days before the performance. I don't know how to move in mine.

COUNTESS. That's exactly why he wants us to get used to them. He says the reason why masked balls take so long to warm up is because everyone is wondering if his trousers are going to fall down.

HERO. There's nothing wrong with my trousers—it's my waistcoat that's too tight. All the same, he did say we could take off our wigs.

COUNTESS. Yes. It's the tyrant's latest whim.

HERO. Pity. It was the part I liked best. My hair is beginning to go.

COUNTESS. You're thirty-seven, Hero.

HERO. I'll be bald at forty. My doctor told me I spend too much time making love. I had a terrible quarrel with him.

HORTENSIA. Because he dared tell you that?

HERO. No. Everyone in Paris knows I'm the original Squire of Dames. He was the one who started the quarrel. He has a beard like a prophet, and as much hair as Absalom. When he told me love makes a man bald, I couldn't help laughing in his face. "Doctor," I said, "I have the impression *you* don't get much fun out of life." He took it very badly. He told me he was married, and father of a family, with more interesting things to do in life. He threatened me with I don't know how many prostates and venereal accidents, and even if I managed to escape on that score, he suggested that I'd get cirrhosis of the liver at least. I rather fancy I was being made to pay for his wife and his Vichy water. The whole thing cost me two thousand francs. You can't amuse yourself quietly any more. You have to pay these people just for telling you that some day you will die.

COUNTESS. You ought to get married, Hero.

HERO. If you can't find me a woman who will make me forget all the others, it would only mean one woman more to satisfy. My strength wouldn't be up to it. And if you could make me fall in love, do you know of any breed of woman who quenches the thirst?

COUNTESS. Hero, you play the cynic, and you're the most sentimental soul in the world. One has only to look at you.

HERO. Your love of paradox leads you astray, Eliane. This deep appealing look in my eyes is nothing but the yearnings of the drunkard. Of course I'm sentimental; but I like causing pain.

COUNTESS. I've never heard anyone really wicked admit that.

HERO. I'm not wicked. I like breaking things. It's a taste small boys lose as they grow up. I have never lost it.

HORTENSIA. When will you make me suffer, Hero? I'm getting impatient.

HERO. Whenever you please, my dear. But it wouldn't amuse either of us. We're too alike.

VILLEBOSSE *enters*.

VILLEBOSSE. Have you heard the news?

HERO. Undoubtedly. We always hear everything before you do.

VILLEBOSSE. Apparently we're to appear without wigs. We'll all look ridiculous!

HERO. I doubt if the wig could have saved you, Villebosse.
He goes to the liqueur cabinet.
May I help myself, Eliane?

COUNTESS. Oh, Hero! We're going to rehearse.

HERO. My talent lies at the bottom of a glass, Eliane—you know that perfectly well. Unfortunately, I don't remember which one. That's why I have to empty so many.

VILLEBOSSE. (*To the* COUNTESS) My dear, that man exasperates me. I will not have him paying his attentions to you.

COUNTESS. You bore me, Villebosse. I didn't take a lover just to listen to reproaches my husband never makes.

VILLEBOSSE. Tiger is a cynic and he doesn't love you. I do. I don't want to precipitate a scandal under your roof, but if that miserable sot allows himself to go too far, I'll slap his face without the least compunction.

COUNTESS. Hero is quite capable of slapping you back and refusing your challenge.

VILLEBOSSE. I'd publish it everywhere! He'd die of shame. He wouldn't dare show his face.

COUNTESS. I don't feel that shame is likely to be the death of Hero. He swallowed shame a long time ago—along with everything else.

VILLEBOSSE. You despise him, at least?

COUNTESS. I don't know.

VILLEBOSSE. For heaven's sake, Eliane. Tell me immediately that you despise him. If you don't, I'll pack my bags and I won't appear in the play.

COUNTESS. If you play such an unkind trick on Tiger, Villebosse, I'll never set eyes on you again.

VILLEBOSSE. Tiger's futilities are the least of my worries. Let him replace me as best he can. I love you, Eliane. I am your lover! Surely that counts for something?

COUNTESS. I'm beginning to find it counts prodigiously. My dear Villebosse, you have succeeded in the paradox of making infidelity more boring than virtue.

VILLEBOSSE. Very well. I shall pretend not to know my part. I will ruin his production! I'm tired of being the only one to suffer!

HERO. *(Returning, glass in hand)* What's Villebosse talking about?

COUNTESS. He says he's suffering.

HERO. How interesting! Hortensia, my little heart of stone, come and look at this gracious natural phenomenon! A man suffering for love. We should never miss a chance of extending our knowledge.

VILLEBOSSE. *(Turning his back)* Sir, I refuse to speak to you.
> *The* COUNT *comes in, holding* LUCILE's *hand, followed by* MONSIEUR DAMIENS *and the* VALET, *who is also in costume.*

COUNT. I have valiantly rescued Silvia from the twelve monsters. *(Sucking his finger)* One tried to claw me. I bleed. . . . Now my children, we can begin. We're all here. *The Double Inconstancy* is a ruthless play. I must beg you not to forget it. Silvia and Harlequin are really in love. The Prince desires Silvia—perhaps he loves her too? Why should princes always be refused the right to love as deeply, as simply, as Harlequin? The whole court will conspire to destroy the loves of Harlequin and Silvia. To snatch Silvia from Harlequin by force, at the Prince's command, would be nothing; but they will try to arrange matters so that Silvia shall fall in love with the Prince, Harlequin will love Flaminia, and they will each forget their first love. In short, it is the story of an elegant and sophisticated crime. Villebosse, Harlequin is tender and good, but easygoing, greedy and simple. Flaminia and her sister are so beautiful, they smell so delicious! Never forget that, even when he rejects them and thinks tenderly of Silvia, he is still conscious of them in his nostrils. The good smell of silk on a scented skin—what a snare for the poor young lad! Flaminia and Lisette, her sister, hard, frivolous, flirtatious, playful; the little rustic must smell good, too, to those fine corrupted ladies. They play with him, show their claws, retract them—desire grows like curiosity—and besides, they are serving their Prince; the iron law of this little world. Why, then, refuse the pleasure of a moment which binds them to nothing? They are creatures of another race, they are well aware of it; and Harlequin is like a dear little dog with an amusing bark and a warm tongue. They let themselves be licked by the little dog, just above the loop of their pearls. It's a new sort of game and hurts nobody. I rather suspect that they have kept their real lovers in reserve. Eliane and Hortensia—I fancy it would be naïve of me to try to give you directions. You will do the whole thing beautifully. (*To* DAMIENS) Trivelin is heavy, anxious to serve, docile and as delighted as a foxhound allowed to join in the kill for his master's credit. He wears court uniform; and it's fine sport to bait the little peasant —the peasant he himself used to be, before he took service. We need not labor the point, but all the same, there's a sort of base and secret joy in the revenge of the poor upon those who are poorer. He has seen it all himself, has been even more humiliated; it's only fair that these two should go through the hoop in their turn; it is simple justice. As for Silvia—(*He turns to* LUCILE) What shall I say of Silvia? She's not romantic, she is tender; she isn't simple, she is good; she isn't hard, she is straightforward. She is dazzled neither by the fine ladies of the court, nor by the Prince. She knows all, has always known all, without ever having learned anything. She is a clear and limpid being. In this luxurious universe, sneering under its silks, its precious stones, its plumes, she stands alone, bright and naked under her cotton frock; erect and silent, she watches them all as they whirl and plot around her. Suddenly, everything which has made for the Prince's strength and pleasure falls to pieces in his hands . . . worthless. Silvia is a small, inaccessible soul who stands watching him, a thousand leagues away, and troubles his heart. So something else besides pleasure exists in this world, something that has always existed . . . and he did not know it?

> *In spite of himself, his voice has changed slightly as he speaks.* HORTENSIA, *the* COUNTESS, *and* HERO *behind his glass look at him in surprise. He breaks off, and ends suddenly, in a low voice.*

COUNT. But I have no need to explain the part to you, mademoiselle. You have only to be yourself.

Everyone is looking at him, motionless.

CURTAIN

SCENE TWO

> *The same. The* COUNT *and* LUCILE, *in costume as before.*

COUNT. I know it's wrong of me to talk to you like this, but I have reached middle age and never yet had the strength to deny myself a pleasure. (*He looks at her and stops*) Forgive me. I have pronounced the unforgivable word. (*He shakes himself*) I don't know what conspiracy of bigots and old maids has managed in two centuries to discredit the word pleasure. It is one of the sweetest and noblest words in the language. I don't believe in God, but if I did, I am sure I should go to Mass with pleasure. Good and evil, in the beginning, must have been what gave pleasure or what did not—as simple as that. The entire moral system of these whited sepulchers rests on that fragile and delicate word they abominate. Why shouldn't love be, above all, a pleasure of the heart? One has all the time in the world to suffer the consequences. (*He looks at her*) In any case, it's enthralling to be in love with a young girl who has lost her tongue. It lures one to soliloquy and meditation. One never talks to oneself enough. Yet one is one's own most attentive listener, the quickest with the right answer. For years now, I haven't said a word to myself. I failed to appreciate myself— I am, in fact, a most agreeable companion. I now discover that I say the wittiest and most unexpected things. How much too quick we always are to judge by appearances. I find my nature both tender and profound.

LUCILE. You know quite well we're supposed to be rehearsing. The others must certainly be listening at the door.

COUNT. The dumb has spoken! How interesting it is when the dumb begin to speak. And—wonder of wonders—it isn't to ask me to be dumb, but merely to ask me to lower my voice.

LUCILE. If I had really wanted to stop you talking any time during the week I have been here, I should have done so. Girls have ways of doing it. Or I could have let you go on talking, and simply not listened. I am just afraid the others may be listening. That's all.

COUNT. Why will you never see me anywhere, except in the drawing room during rehearsals? What game are you playing, assuming I don't bore you?

LUCILE. No game at all, I promise. When I do fall in love with a man, the moment I'm sure of it, I shall do everything I can to give him pleasure—as you called it. I shall be entirely his at once, without playing any game.

COUNT. I wonder what virtues or what guarantees you'll expect from that important person?

LUCILE. None. I shall belong to him, even if he's poor, an outcast, even if he doesn't know where he'll sleep at night; even if he has a wife and children, and can only spare one hour a week when we can meet in a café.

COUNT. (*With a trace of temper*) You all surround yourselves with mysteries, and you're all alike! Particularly if he's poor, of course—particularly if he's an outcast! If you're not taken by force, then you always need a touch of pity for a man before you'll give yourselves.

LUCILE. (*Gently*) Even if he is rich and happy. It's exactly the same thing.

COUNT. Very well! I am rich and happy and I want you to love me.

LUCILE. Little children also cry for the moon. It's my job to explain that they can't have it so easily. You believe I don't want to love you? You or anybody else? It must be so wonderful to give everything.

COUNT. Mustn't it? And it all fits in beautifully, because I am a beggar. We ought to be able to arrange things between us.

LUCILE. My poor monsieur—one can only give to the rich.

COUNT. Explain yourself, if you please. I always came last in Divinity—I could never make head or tail of the parables.

LUCILE. The boy who loves me as I want to be loved, won't need to ask.

COUNT. How will you know he loves you? Because he tells you so, poor bird?

LUCILE. No. Because he probably won't even think of telling me. And certainly not so amusingly as you do.

COUNT. What will this paragon do? Talk about the moon? Sigh and groan? Throw himself on his knees, pounding himself over the putative region of the heart?

LUCILE. He'll be shy. I don't suppose he'll say a word. He may even avoid my eyes. He will ask another girl to dance, but I shall know I'm the one he really loves.

COUNT. (*After a slight pause*) The rules seem a trifle complicated. But I shall learn. I'm very good at all games.

LUCILE. I'm afraid this one can't be taught.

COUNT. When I am in love, I want to be lovable—dazzling—I want to shine. Cocks ruffle their feathers. It must be a natural reaction.

LUCILE. Above all, I shall want the boy I love not to be able to find exactly the right word when he loves me . . . I hope he will be as startled as I. But please let's rehearse. We are gossiping and we'll never be ready. It would be terrible, wouldn't it, if we didn't know our parts?

COUNT. Very well. Thank you for putting me so gently in my place. I'm an ass. As a boy, I was somewhat spoiled by fortune; and I have plenty of bad habits, it's true. Forget the whole thing and let's rehearse. You're quite right.

He begins.

"How's this, Silvia? You will not look at me . . ."

He stops.

One word more. I'm a poor devil, of course, and it must be marvelous to be simple and give everything. It's a gift I was never endowed with, that's all. You're an adorable child beneath your light veil of mist, for the man with eyes to see. During the week you've been here, I've been asking myself why I can think of nothing but you. I've told you as much—in my own way—that is, under cover of my wit. You've made it clear that either the matter or the manner fails to please you. Good. I've been well brought up. I shan't chase you down the corridors, trying to put my arm around your waist. Neither shall I throw myself in the pond. Between those two extremes there is a golden mean: mere regret for the loss of a charming adventure, nothing more.

Let us rehearse. As you say, people might overhear us. I've been quite absurd enough for one evening, and there's no point in letting it go any further.
> *He begins.*

"How's this, Silvia? You will not look at me? Each time that I accost you, you grow sad. It grieves me to suppose myself importunate."

LUCILE. (*Looking at him and smiling*) You're very sweet, all the same.

COUNT. Sweet?

LUCILE. You're still the little boy with his white gloves, his stick and his very first bowler hat who took his constitutional every morning in the Avenue du Bois.

COUNT. What? Who told you that? In the days of my first bowler, you were still puling in your cot, little girl.

LUCILE. That doesn't matter. I can just see you! It's difficult to grow up, isn't it? But please—let's rehearse.

COUNT. It's most disconcerting! You look at me kindly for the first time, and for what? To drown me in your pity. No one's ever played that trick on me before! Yes, I did wear a bowler—I was a little too young for it, perhaps, but it happened to be all the fashion. Yes, I did go for a stroll in the Avenue du Bois before lunch, every morning, but I lived close by, and all my friends did the same. I don't think I was so absurd, so far as I can remember. . . . At any rate, the girls of your age—in those days—didn't think so. And I really don't see what there is about me that gives you the right to treat me like an ass!

LUCILE. You mustn't lose your temper. It's rather good to have remained a real little boy.

COUNT. But I'm not a little boy! I've been through the war. I had a cannon—a real cannon. They gave me a medal, as they do to children, of course, but I never wear it. For fifteen years I have given the most successful balls in Paris—grown-up ones, too. I drive a car, I have even raced them. At one time I was a diplomat, and if I'd stuck it out, I might be representing France somewhere or other at this very moment. I don't know what else to tell you! I'm a man like other men—rather more brilliant than other men, or so I'm told—I'm tired of listening to your tiny fluting like a great subjugated snake. Let us rehearse. "How's this, Silvia? You will not look at me? Each time that I accost you, you grow sad."

LUCILE. (*Placidly taking her place to begin rehearsing*) You know, what I say isn't very important. If you start listening to the chatter of girls, you'll be dreadfully misled. . . . Treat me as I deserve. I shan't take offense . . .

COUNT. (*Still in a temper*) But I'm not listening to you! I am merely astonished. Come on, come on—rehearse. I am making a fool of myself, and *you're* playing a game, whatever you say, and playing it a good deal more wittily than I am. I know how to be a good loser—that, also, is part of my excellent upbringing. But don't go around boasting about it. That's all I ask.

LUCILE. Boasting? To whom?

COUNT. How should I know? To your godfather—your girl friends . . .

LUCILE. I never speak to my godfather. You must have noticed that there's not much love lost between us. And I have no girl friends.

COUNT. Good. To your twelve little orphans, perhaps.

LUCILE. Oh, I shall tell them, of course. I have to tell them so many magical stories every night to send them to sleep. I've just exhausted my stock of fairy tales. . . . But I shall change the context. This will all take place in the Middle Ages. Besides, they never understand anything—they're asleep long before the end.

COUNT. (*Beginning again*) Splendid. Let us rehearse. "How's this, Silvia? You will not look at me? Each time that I accost you, you grow sad. It grieves me to suppose myself importunate."

LUCILE. "Importunate? I was speaking of you only just now!"

COUNT. "Speaking of me? And what, fair Silvia, did you say?"

LUCILE. "Oh, I said many things. I said that you don't yet know what I am thinking."

COUNT. "I know you are resolved to refuse me your heart, and thereby I know your thoughts."

LUCILE. "You are not so clever as you think. Do not boast so much. But tell me—for you are an honest man and I am sure you will tell me the truth. You know that I am here with Harlequin. For the moment, let us suppose I have a longing to love you. If I satisfied that longing, should I be doing well, or ill? There. Give me your counsel, in all good faith."

COUNT. "One cannot be master of one's heart. Therefore, if you desire to love me, you would do well to follow that desire. That is my opinion."

LUCILE. "Are you speaking to me as a friend?"

COUNT. "Yes, Silvia, and with all my heart."

LUCILE. "I share your opinions. I have just come to the same conclusion and I believe we are both right—so I am resolved to love you if I please, and he shall not have the smallest word to say."

COUNT. "Thereby I gain nothing, for he does not please you at all."

LUCILE. "Do not try to guess . . ."

COUNT. (*Interrupting suddenly*) That's it, of course! It's perfectly simple. You lied to me—you do love someone. Some little man who also goes in for kinderculture. You write him a four-page letter every night before you go to sleep.

LUCILE. I don't think you are keeping to the lines.

COUNT. I must ask you one question. Give me a straight answer. The others are coming.

LUCILE. (*Looks at him and says gravely*) No. I am not in love, and I have never been in love with anyone.

The others come in.

COUNTESS. Well—how goes the last scene?

COUNT. Extremely well. We think we're both very talented.

COUNTESS. We others, who are not so gifted, had better rehearse too.

COUNT. Would you like to go through the whole play? Monsieur Damiens says he's still very shaky.

COUNTESS. Monsieur Damiens is used to speaking in public. In the days when he appeared at the Assizes, there was never a dry eye in the house. He will certainly get on much better than all of us.

M. DAMIENS. We shall see. I was very young in those days,

madame. I was far less ashamed to put a quaver into my voice. Besides, I wore great wide sleeves and I wrote my own lines.

COUNTESS. Don't belittle yourself, Monsieur Damiens, and don't start overacting just to get a second hearing. I have no fears for you. Besides, we haven't time to go through the whole play before dinner. We can do that this evening.

COUNT. In that case, let's start with the beginning of the second act. We can cut Silvia's long speeches. My dear Hortensia, we are doing this for your benefit. I think you are a little too acid in your scene with Silvia. You are underlining too much. Be charming, as I know you can. You have to deceive the girl, remember.

HORTENSIA. (*Immediately taking offense*) If you don't think I'm up to the part, my dear Tiger . . .

COUNT. Hortensia, it fits you like a glove! I am merely asking for a trifle more subtlety. Actors are the most impossible people. As soon as they open their mouths, the sound of their own voices affects them like a snake charmer's flute. They grow quite stupefied with the pleasure of listening to themselves and have a cast-iron belief that we're sharing their ecstasy. In the theatre, my dear, the natural, the true, is the least natural thing in the world. Don't make the mistake of believing it's enough to reproduce the realities of life. Besides, in real life the script is always so unsatisfactory. We live in a world that has completely lost the use of the semicolon; we all talk in broken sentences, ending in three little dots, because we can never find the exact word. And then, the natural conversational tone, which actors pretend to reproduce; these babblings, these hiccoughs, these hesitations, these droolings—it really isn't worth inveigling five or six hundred people into a theatre and asking them to pay for the privilege, merely to give them such an exhibition. They love it, I know, because they recognize themselves. Which doesn't make it less true that one should write and act better than that. Life is all very well, but it has no construction. The object of art is to give life a shape, and to do it by every conceivable artifice—to make it more real than reality. But I'm boring you. I'm beginning to take myself seriously. Beginning Act Two. Silvia, you speak.

LUCILE. (*To* HORTENSIA) "Yes, I believe you. You seem to wish me well, but you may perceive that I am suffering as cruelly as you. I regard the others as my enemies. But where is Harlequin?"

HORTENSIA. "He will come soon—he is still dining."

HERO. (*Into his glass, glancing at* VILLEBOSSE, *sulking in his corner*) Wrong! He's not dining, he's suffering. If he seems to be dining, it's because he's chewing the cud of his spite.

VILLEBOSSE. Monsieur, I have already told you I'm not speaking to you! My patience has its limits, you know!

COUNT. Hero—do be serious for once.

HERO. Impossible, dear boy—I'm not drunk yet. I'll be serious later.

LUCILE. "There is something frightening about this country! Never have I seen women so well-bred, or men so courteous. Their manners are delightful, so many courtesies, so many compliments, so many marks of friendship! You would say they were the best people on earth, that they were full of goodness and sensibility. What an error of judgment!"
 To the COUNT.
Shall I cut?

COUNT. Yes, yes. Cut. You say all that very well. . . .
He looks at LUCILE's *script.*
"To be worthless . . ."

LUCILE. "To be worthless, to deceive their neighbors, to break their plighted word, to cheat, to lie! That's what they want, the ladies and gentlemen of this accursed place. What can these people be? Where do they come from? Of what clay are they made?"

HORTENSIA. "The same clay as other men, my dear Silvia, which shouldn't surprise you. They believe the Prince's marriage will make for your happiness."

LUCILE. "But am I not required to be faithful? Is it not my duty as an honest girl? And when one fails in one's duty, can one be happy? Besides, is not this fidelity my touchstone?"
To the COUNT.
Shall I cut?

COUNT. No. I'm enjoying it too much. Go on.

LUCILE. "And none of them has the courage to say: There—play an evil trick which will bring you nothing but harm—throw away your joy and your integrity! And because I refuse, they call me obstinate."

HORTENSIA. "What do you expect? These people think in their own fashion, desire nought but happiness for their Prince."

COUNT. Good, Hortensia!

LUCILE. "But why does the Prince not take some girl who would give herself willingly? How strange a fancy to want the very one who does not want him! What pleasure can he find in that?"

COUNTESS. (*To the* COUNT *at whom* LUCILE *has been looking*) Tell her the Prince isn't on stage, Tiger. She must look at Hortensia.

LUCILE. "Everything he does is wrong. All these concerts, these plays, these great meals just like wedding breakfasts, these jewels he sends me! It's costing him a fortune. It's a bottomless pit. He's ruining himself. Ask me what he seeks to gain! If he loaded me with the entire contents of a jeweler's shop, it wouldn't please me half so much as the skein of wool that Harlequin gave me."

HORTENSIA. "No doubt of it. That is true love. I, too, have loved like that. And I, too, have preferred a skein of wool."
To the COUNT.
Does she mean it when she says that? I feel I sound insincere. Has she ever really been in love? Did she really once prefer a little skein of wool to all the Prince's jewels?

COUNT. What about you, Hortensia dear?

HORTENSIA. Tiger, it's nothing to do with me. If this is a game you're playing, it isn't funny. You've just told us we mustn't be ourselves . . .

COUNT. Forgive me. When I cast the play, I knew quite well what I was doing. You said that line perfectly.

HORTENSIA. I tried to make it sincere.

COUNT. Since you've never preferred a small skein of wool to your own pleasures, in saying the line "sincerely," you sounded abominably false. It was perfect. Just what I wanted. Go on.

HORTENSIA. You're treating us all like puppets. You'll exhaust our patience soon.

COUNT. All directors of real genius do that. You can be grateful I don't go in for shouting and tearing up the script. Hysterics are the hallmark of the production of genius. Insults are its common currency; some of the really great directors go so far as physical violence. And don't believe it's done for nothing! It always shows in performance if the director has really cracked the whip. A play produced by a man with good manners very rarely shows genius. Go on, Silvia—go on. "Ah well! let him try to forget me then."

LUCILE. "Ah well! Let him try to forget me then, send me away, turn to another. . . . There are many here who have their lovers as I do, but that doesn't stop them loving other people. I'm aware that it means nothing to them. But for me, it's impossible."

HORTENSIA. "My dear child, have we anyone here to match you in beauty and virtue?"

COUNT. Excellent!—the poison beneath the smile. You must have worked all night to get that so exactly, Hortensia!

LUCILE. "Oh, but you have! There are many fairer than I and even were they half as pretty, they know better than I how to make the most of their beauty. I have seen ugly people here who make such beautiful faces that one is quite deceived."

COUNTESS. It's Flaminia you're looking at, my child. I'm not on stage yet—my entrance comes later.

HORTENSIA. "Yes, but your beauty is natural, and that is so charming."

LUCILE. "Mine! Oh, that's as you please. I shan't wager on it. I am nothing beside the others. I shall not change; I am as I am. They always seem happy. Their eyes caress the whole world; their bearing is bold, their beauty free, unembarrassed, unaffected. They must be far more attractive than a humble girl like me who dares not raise her eyes, and blushes when someone finds her beautiful."

COUNTESS. I feel she ought to say that line more modestly. Don't you think so, Tiger? She looks as though she's attacking in her turn.

COUNT. But of course she is attacking—she attacks! Everybody's beginning to want her to attack!

COUNTESS. Besides, Mademoiselle is charming—we all think so; so far as I'm concerned, I feel you were quite right to give her the part. All the same—I can say it in front of her, because I know she's very intelligent—she hasn't quite enough glamour to justify the confidence in her own beauty which shows in the text. She should say the line more simply.

COUNT. I don't agree with you. I think she says it quite perfectly. Go on, Hortensia.

HORTENSIA. "But that's precisely what has moved the Prince! It's what he admires! Such innocence, such beauty unadorned, such natural grace. And if you'll take a hint from me, don't praise these ladies so generously, because they will not return the compliment."

LUCILE. "What do they say about me?"

HORTENSIA. "Impertinences. They make fun of you, tease the Prince, ask him for news of his rustic beauty. Was there ever so commonplace a countenance? said those jealous ones the other day. So gawky a manner? Thereupon one dispraised your eyes, another your lips. Even the men had some fault to find with you. Oh, it put me in such a fury!"

LUCILE. "Lud! What wretches they must be, denying their real opinions to please all those idiots!"

COUNT. Isn't she amusing? Don't you think she's amusing when she says that? I adore this little character.

HORTENSIA. "It takes little to please them." Don't interrupt all the time, Tiger—it's maddening. "It takes little to please them."

LUCILE. "How I hate such women! But since their opinion of me is so low, why does the Prince love me, and abandon them?"

HORTENSIA. "Oh, they're convinced he will not love you long; that it's merely a passing fancy, that he'll leave you all the sooner."

COUNT. Heavens, how well you said that, Hortensia! You've got it, my dear, you've only to carry on like that. Let's cut the rest and go on to my entrance with Eliane. That's very important. (*He takes the* COUNTESS's *arm*) Come along, Eliane—our cue.

LUCILE. "What, is it you, sir? Were you then aware of my presence here?"

COUNT. "Yes, mademoiselle. But you commanded me to see you no more and I should never have dared to show myself without Madame, who desired me to accompany her and has obtained from her Prince the honor of making you a curtsy."

LUCILE. "I am not angry at seeing you, but you find me in low spirits. As for this lady, I thank her for her kindness in wishing to make me a curtsy. I do not deserve it, but she may do so if she pleases. I shall do the same, to the best of my ability. She will pardon me if I do it clumsily."

COUNTESS. "Indeed, my dear, I will pardon you with all my heart. I do not ask you to perform the impossible."

LUCILE. "To perform the impossible! What a thing to say!"

COUNTESS. "Child, how old are you?"

LUCILE. "Mother, I have forgotten."

HORTENSIA. (*To* LUCILE) "Bravo!"

COUNTESS. "She is angry, I think."

COUNT. "Madame, what is the meaning of this exchange? Under pretext of paying your respects to Silvia, you insult her?"

COUNTESS. "Such was not my intention. But I was curious to see this child, who inspires such a love, who arouses so fierce a passion, and to find out for myself what makes her so desirable. They say she's naïve—there's a rustic charm about that which ought to be amusing. Ask her to give us a taste of her simplicity. Let us judge of her wit."

LUCILE. "Oh, dear me, no, madame! It isn't worth the trouble. My wit is not so sprightly as yours."

HORTENSIA. "Ah! Ah! You asked for simplicity—and here it is!"

COUNT. (*To the* COUNTESS) "Leave us, madame."

COUNTESS. "I shall be out of patience soon. If she doesn't go, I shall go myself at once."

COUNT. (*To the* COUNTESS) "You will answer to me for your actions."

COUNTESS. "Farewell! Such a choice revenges me enough upon the chooser."

COUNT. Perfect. Scene Three.

THE REHEARSAL

COUNTESS. (*Carrying on—almost on the same tone*) Enough. I'm tired, Tiger, and I'd like to have a word with you. Will you please come up to my room?

HORTENSIA. Good idea— Let's stop for a while. Tiger finds it all tremendously amusing—I don't think we enjoy it so much. We all need a breathing space, my dear.

COUNT. Very well—we'll stop. The rehearsal will start again in fifteen minutes.

    HORTENSIA *has gone out.*

(*To* HERO) My dear Hero, women don't understand the theatre. It's no fun for them to be anything but themselves.

HERO. They should take to drink—that makes all games amusing. You too, Villebosse.

    VILLEBOSSE *turns, exasperated.*

VILLEBOSSE. One day, sir, I'll suggest a game you'll find far less amusing.

COUNTESS. (*From the doorway*) Well, Tiger? Are you coming?

VILLEBOSSE. (*Getting up, suspiciously*) Where will you be, Eliane?

COUNTESS. I don't know. You bore me, Villebosse.
    They have all gone out, the COUNT *shrugging his shoulders.* VILLEBOSSE *is worried.*

    LUCILE, DAMIENS *and* HERO *remain.*

HERO. (*Going out, glass in hand, crosses to* LUCILE) Mademoiselle, your performance is quite exquisite. That's the opinion of a drunk; I drank in every word. I was so absorbed the whole time, I forgot to drink anything else. Tomorrow, I shall write and tell my doctor and doubtless he will send you a note of thanks. I'm going to get out of this rig. My waistcoat is too tight. Although I've never touched a drop of water in my life, they tell me I have gallons of it in my belly. . . . Life is full of such curious contradictions. You didn't know that yet, did you, dear heart?

He has come a little too close to LUCILE *as he speaks. She draws back imperceptibly.*

You draw away? I smell, perhaps? I smell of alcohol. What else do you expect me to smell of? But it isn't such a bad smell. They pickle the livers of famous drunkards in alcohol to frighten good little boys. Do I frighten you?

LUCILE. No.

HERO. That's because you can't see my liver. Apparently it's an appalling efflorescence. A virgin forest of many-colored blossoms. I see you don't like flowers. That's all right. No doubt I disgust you?

She does not reply. He is very close to her, glass in hand. He smiles maliciously.

That's all right too. I ought to disgust you a little. It's in my part. Not my part in the Marivaux—the other—the one I play in real life.

On his way to the door, he passes close to DAMIENS.

Your goddaughter is quite charming, Monsieur Damiens, but if, instead of being called Hero de . . . I won't bother you with my name, it is much too long—I were simple Monsieur Damiens, I swear to you I'd take her out of here. (*He smiles mysteriously from the doorway*) Word of a drunkard!

He has finally gone. LUCILE *seems to shiver a little in disgust and turns to go.* MONSIEUR DAMIENS *makes a gesture to stop her.*

M. DAMIENS. I must talk to you, Lucile.

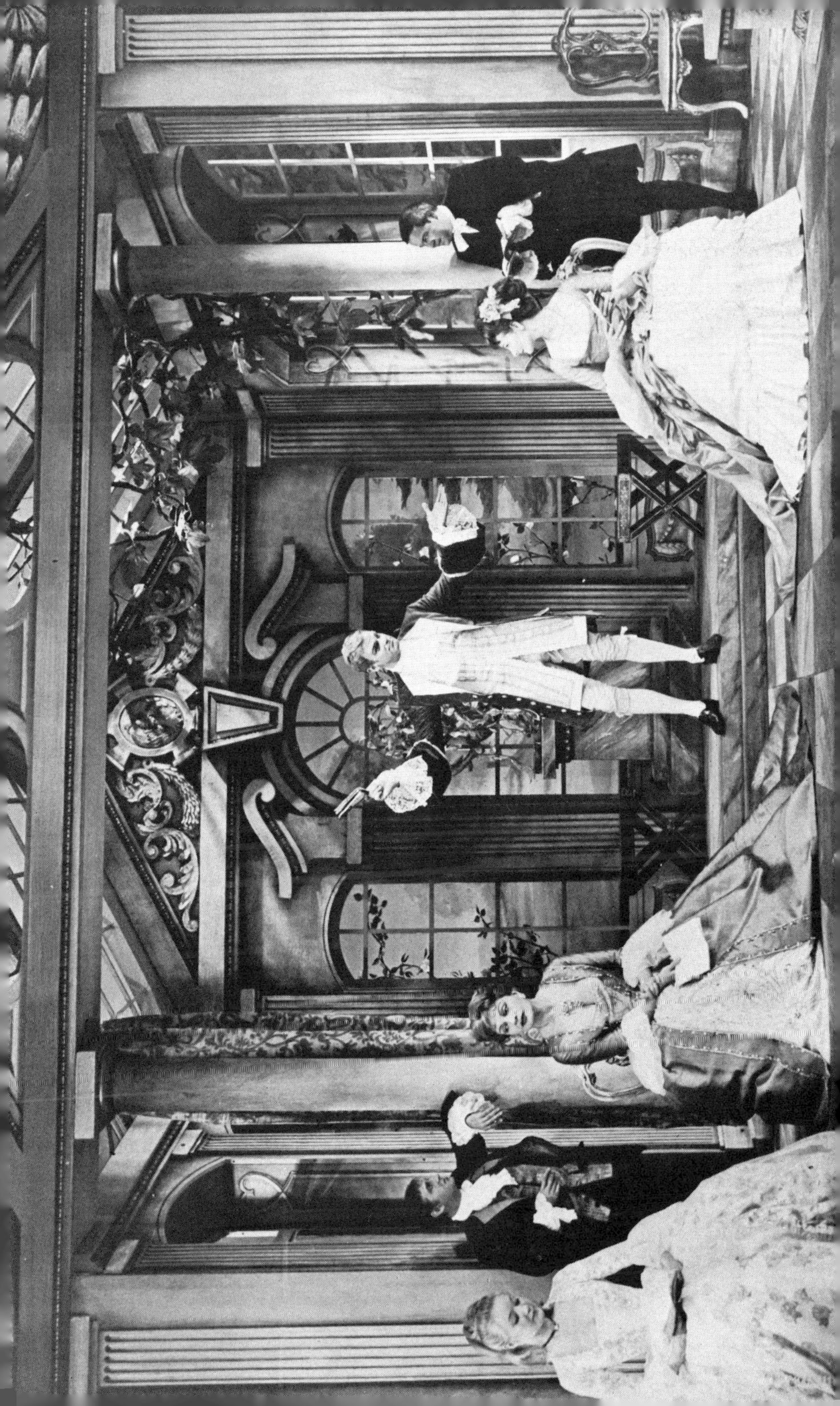

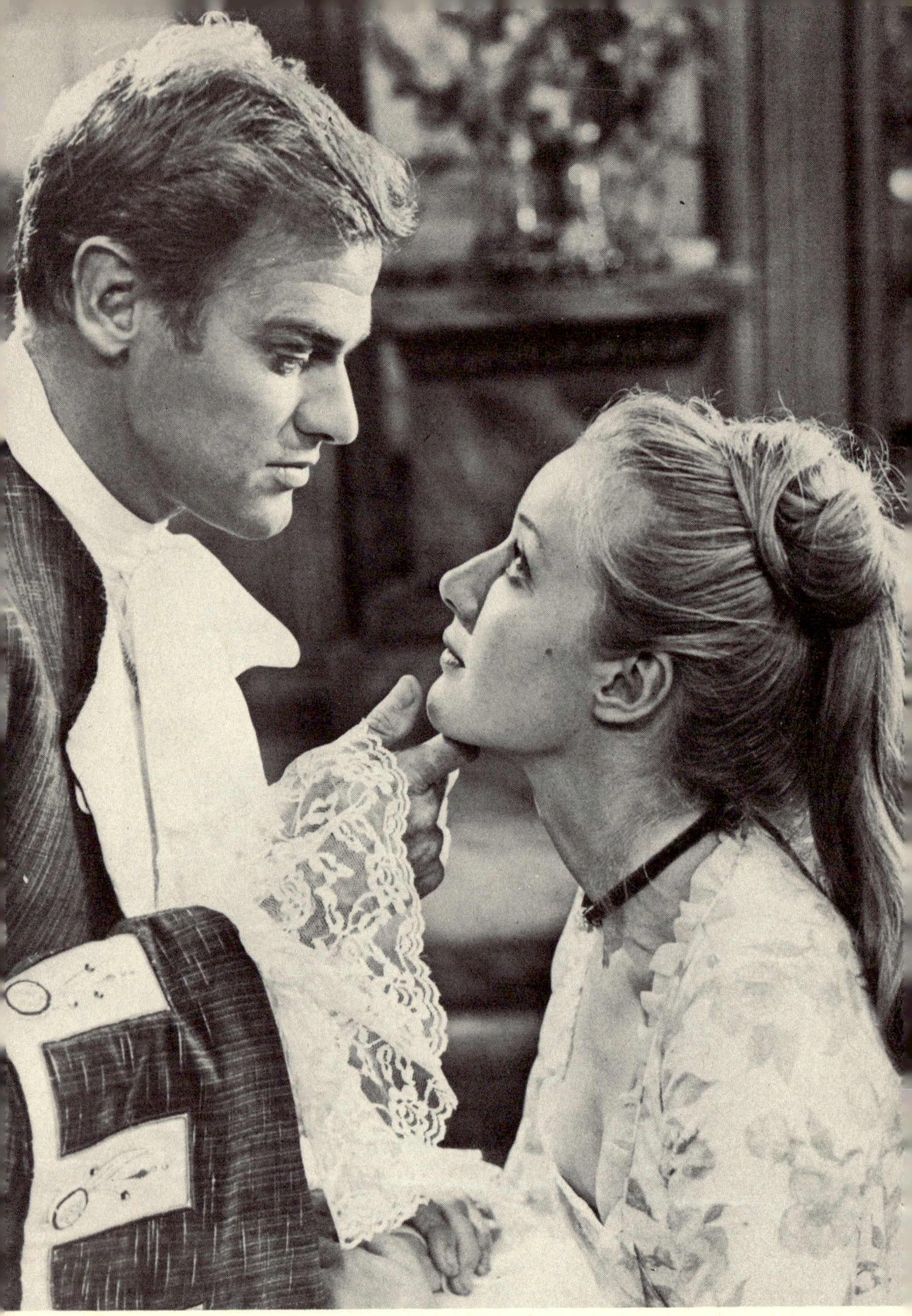

LUCILE. (*Reserved*) I'm listening.

M. DAMIENS. You are young. You do not know much of the world, nor of life. When your poor mother died, you wished to work in order to be independent, and that showed the right spirit. All the same, you know, you weren't obliged . . .

LUCILE. Not obliged? Mother lived on her widow's pension. When she died, I was left with a Renaissance dining table, three Regency chairs we always thought were real but which turned out to be fakes, my gramophone and an old cat. What else could I do?

M. DAMIENS. I was there.

LUCILE. You are my godfather, of course. It was very kind of you to take an interest in me. But I did not want to owe you anything.

M. DAMIENS. (*Gently*) Why not, Lucile?

LUCILE. You know why not.

M. DAMIENS. My proposal seemed monstrous to you at first sight. God knows what a girl of eighteen dreams of. . . . That's why I left you alone. I wanted life and hard work to teach you a little sad wisdom, to show you what they have to offer in reality. I know these two years have been very hard for you.

LUCILE. Have I complained?

M. DAMIENS. Never, no, for you have a great deal of pride. But do you think I liked watching you struggling at the end of the month, with the little hat you had retrimmed a hundred times? With your gloves in holes and your worn-out stockings? You are pretty, and I know that at your age a girl wants pretty clothes. I should have liked to have made things easier for you.

LUCILE. I should have liked it too—I'm no heroine. But not from you.

M. DAMIENS. You are alone in the world. I had the right—I should have thought. The duty, even . . .

LUCILE. Please don't begin this conversation all over again—You know it distresses me. When I was a child you bought me dolls and sewing baskets—then you found this position for me. You have more than done your duty. Now I can manage alone.

M. DAMIENS. Why won't you let me give you the security you need?

LUCILE. At my age, one doesn't ask for security.

M. DAMIENS. I don't mean just material security. I mean—a sincere affection. Care. Protection.

LUCILE. (*Looking at him squarely*) Whom will you protect me against, if I accept your proposition? Against other men who might propose the same thing as yourself?

M. DAMIENS. (*Coming to her, a little more sharply*) Against less worthy men, without the love and respect I have for you. Men who might think only of an evening's enjoyment.

LUCILE. Haven't you learned that I know how to protect myself?

M. DAMIENS. Perhaps against me. I was honest enough to tell you what I was offering. But against another, younger and more attractive, who would lie to you . . .

LUCILE. If he were younger and more attractive it would at any rate be less depressing, even if it didn't last so long.

Particularly if it didn't last so long. It is better for shame not to stretch into one's whole future. And at least the enjoyment might be mutual.

M. DAMIENS. I can't bear to hear you speak so cynically. I am sorry now that I brought you into this house!

LUCILE. Because they put me into costume and make me act a part for the same salary? In my situation I know one has to accept certain things. . . . The matron of the children's home where I first went to work, taught me I had to sing for my supper. I know my place. And if that's what you hoped life would teach me, the lesson has been learned.

M. DAMIENS. My dear child, the Count wants you, and he won't stop till he gets what he wants. Everyone here has seen what he's up to. You must have noticed it yourself during that rehearsal? The Countess is a clever woman. She overlooks his mistresses as he, for his part, overlooks her lovers, provided the game is played within their own world, with cards she recognizes. She will never let him pay court to you. She'll heap you with humiliations. Send you packing.

LUCILE. Is that what you're so afraid of? That I might lose my job? I should go to another children's home, that's all. There is one thing you don't know: how rich one can be when one has nothing to lose. All children are alike. They all scream, make the same little messes at the same inconvenient moments, clamor for the same kisses at night from the little girl, hardly bigger than themselves, who is paid to pretend she is their mother.

M. DAMIENS. You couldn't be that man's mistress!

LUCILE. Don't be afraid—I shan't. But for quite different reasons, which only concern me.

M. DAMIENS. He's making a fool of you. He's a libertine . . . a . . .

The COUNT *comes in abruptly. He is a little pale.*

COUNT. Forgive me, Monsieur Damiens, I must carry off your goddaughter again. I have a scene with her to put right before this evening's rehearsal. Will you excuse me?

M. DAMIENS. (*Stiffly*) I place her in your care, Monsieur le Comte. I have just been putting her on guard against the temptations of a world and a life which are not her own. It was a charming idea to cast her in your comedy, and I am very grateful to you, and to Madame la Comtesse, for being so good as to treat her as an equal; but I do not wish her to forget that she is here to earn her living and to look after the children.

COUNT. My dear Damiens! On the contrary I shall do my best to try and make her forget it. It can't be such a source of amusement that she has to remember it all the time. And if I must take care of something, I shall take care to see that people don't remind her of it. Mademoiselle Lucile is my guest. If, in addition to the honor she has done us in agreeing to act (with far more talent than we) in this comedy of Marivaux, she is brave enough and kind enough to look after my aunt's little monsters (instead of sleeping till midday like the other ladies and primping before her looking glass) that is yet another reason why we should respect her. I hope to make that clear to everyone.

M. DAMIENS. If you will be good enough to undertake that task yourself, then I shall leave you, completely reassured. Sir.

MONSIEUR DAMIENS *bows and goes out.*

COUNT. (*Turning toward* LUCILE) No—don't say anything. First of all, I owe you an apology. All my life, I've been surrounded by charming cads; I've grown so used to it that I've probably become one myself. Before the performance, there's nothing to be done . . . an entertainment is an entertainment, and this one has to be given. . . . They will all make your life unbearable, but I know you're a brave girl. I have just had a conversation with my wife, and I—who thought I knew everything—have just discovered how far a woman of taste and intelligence can let herself go in baseness and stupidity when she feels something unusual and dangerous in the air. For they have all realized that I love you, and that it isn't a caprice. So this is what I propose. Say nothing, please, until I have finished. It must be obvious to you that I can't agree to go on with my pleasant, trivial life of pleasure while you, somewhere in this vast world, are busy blowing children's noses and cleaning up after them—children who aren't even your own. You're worth more than that—worth more than anything I can offer you.

> *With a gesture he stops her from speaking and continues.*

I have very little money—you can rest easy on that score. I swallowed up my inheritance many moons ago, but by selling the few heirlooms that remain to me, I can raise enough to take you abroad. You can go back to your studies, without having to go on with this idiotic work—you'll be free, and I shall hope with all my heart that within a few years, or a few months, you will find a lad of your own age worthy of you, who will help you to build a proper life. I shall never see you again.

> *Pause. He adds:*

I can see the talk of money embarrasses you, but unfortunately one can't avoid it. Money means nothing to free souls—it's a meaningless symbol. One mustn't be too middle-class about money—I merely ask you very humbly to share what I have left. You can leave the day after the performance.
    Another pause. He concludes:
Of course, this is the proposition of an egoist. An egoist who has never held you in his arms, not even once, and who is very unhappy. (*He asks very humbly*) Will you agree?

LUCILE. (*Looks at him*) No. Of course not.
    He looks at her, bewildered. She adds gently:
Now, I would rather stay.
    He looks at her for a moment, hesitating, then takes her suddenly in his arms and kisses her.

COUNT. My little girl.

LUCILE. (*Nestling in his arms*) It's so wonderful! Is this what they call tenderness? I thought that only came much later on.

COUNT. I thought so too. We must have been very quick.

LUCILE. We've done it properly. This is the right way . . .
    They are in each other's arms. She murmurs suddenly:
I'm afraid.

COUNT. Of what?

LUCILE. That I won't be able to please you for long. I'm not beautiful.

COUNT. You are.

LUCILE. Not like Hortensia.

COUNT. No. Thank goodness.

LUCILE. I'm not clever.

COUNT. Are you stupid enough to want me to say yes?

LUCILE. In any case, I can never think of anything funny to say at the right time.

COUNT. I should hope not.

LUCILE. I'm poor. It's not the condition that's serious, it's the habit. I dress badly and if I had any money for clothes, I might dress myself even worse. You have only to look at my hands to see that I'm no stranger to the washing-tub and even to the washtub—anyway, that I've had to work with my hands. What is there in me to make you love me, once the novelty has worn off?

COUNT. (*Gently*) Not being beautiful like the others, being awkward, being poor; not to have painted claws cluttered with flashy stones (*Takes her hand*) but two little bare hands with short nails, hard-working hands. (*He takes them and kisses them*) Hands of a real woman.

LUCILE. (*Murmurs*) If I thought it was just a fancy for beggar maids which attracts you, I'd be so ashamed I should die.

COUNT. It would be foolish of you not to understand, you who understand everything always. Do you suppose it was only by accident that all the old legends are about captive princes hungrily searching for poor maidens to set them free? And don't you suppose they found it easy? The world is full of shopgirls ready to adore princes, whatever they're like.

LUCILE. Everyone will believe that's why I love you.

COUNT. Be sure they'll play that for all they're worth to drive us apart. But do you believe it? Do you?

LUCILE. No.

COUNT. Neither do I. Don't be silly. Well, if neither of us believes it, who is this "everyone" you're babbling about? Show me!

LUCILE. (*Softly, indicating the others, who are coming in*) Why, there!

COUNT. Walk-ons, that's all. Small parts in this private play we're going to act together.
He continues in a loud voice.
"Yes, Silvia, I have concealed my rank from you until this moment in order to awaken your love only by mine, nothing more. I could not bear to lose the joy it might bring me. Now you know who I am, you are at liberty to accept my hand and heart or to reject them both," etc. etc. . . .
He turns to the others.
You're all very punctual, thank you. I hope you had a good rest. If you don't mind, before we go though the play again, we might turn our attention to an important item. Professional actors never forget to rehearse it before the first night. They spend all the time necessary on it, even if the play itself isn't quite perfect. I mean the curtain calls. This is what I suggest and what seems to me most logical. I give my hand to Lucile, with Eliane on my right, then Hero, then Hortensia: Damiens on Lucile's left, then, Villebosse . . .
He looks for him.
Where's Villebosse?

VILLEBOSSE *enters, furious as usual.*

VILLEBOSSE. They told me we were going to rehearse on the terrace! It's four o'clock. Do we rehearse or do we not?

COUNT. Just a second, Villebosse. For the moment, we're going to do something even more important in the theatre. Take our calls.

> *They bow to the public in the order the Count has indicated.*

CURTAIN

Act Two

The same. The COUNTESS *and* HORTENSIA *on stage.* HORTENSIA *is seated, the* COUNTESS *pacing up and down nervously, in silence.* VILLEBOSSE *enters.*

VILLEBOSSE. Now look here. Do we rehearse or do we not?

COUNTESS. You're disturbing us, Villebosse.

HORTENSIA. Tiger insisted on us being dressed by four o'clock. He's keeping us waiting.

VILLEBOSSE. What on earth has been going on since yesterday? We rehearse without any expression—or else give certain lines far too much, as if they were charged with overtones that quite escape me. Everyone sniggers suddenly and nobody knows why; everyone insults everyone else; the little girl's in tears, Tiger blushes scarlet and leaves the rehearsal. . . . Today we're starting an hour late. We have to give a performance in three days' time and I have an enormous part. I won't be made to look ridiculous.

COUNTESS. Go away, Villebosse. I want to talk to Hortensia.

VILLEBOSSE. Eliane, I don't understand you, either. The way you treat me is utterly baffling. What on earth have I done?

COUNTESS. Nothing. Absolutely nothing. That's the whole point. Leave us alone.

VILLEBOSSE. But I'm suffering, Eliane!

COUNTESS. Then go and suffer in the garden. I want to talk to Hortensia. We'll call you back later.

VILLEBOSSE. I don't see what I've done to make you turn against me.

COUNTESS. My poor boy, it's nothing to do with you. I'm asking you to leave us alone for a moment, that's all.

VILLEBOSSE. I'll leave you, but I'm at the end of my patience. I'll wait on the terrace till you call. You owe me an explanation.

COUNTESS. You'll get it. We'll all get it.

VILLEBOSSE *goes out.*

My dear Hortensia, I don't understand you! For goodness' sake! He's courting this girl; he's mad about her—it's obvious to the meanest intelligence. He's even forgotten about his entertainment, and it's the first time in my life that I've known Tiger to neglect his pleasure. And you can stand there, doing nothing!

HORTENSIA. I think he's revolting!

COUNTESS. It's no use finding him revolting and not lifting a finger. Good God, if I were Tiger's mistress, I shouldn't let myself be made a fool of like this. Hortensia, you disappoint me.

HORTENSIA. You know as well as I do that if we had a scene it wouldn't settle anything.

COUNTESS. You aren't suggesting that I should have the scene myself? I didn't have one over you. I have no reason to have one with him over this child.

HORTENSIA. Let's leave him alone. He'll manage to get into her room tonight, and tomorrow he won't give her another thought.

COUNTESS. Hortensia, you're blind. Tiger isn't the same any more. Something has been touched in him that nothing has been able to reach before. I was watching him yesterday, during dinner; he looked like a snapshot of himself one of his comrades took during the war, the morning of the German offensive—a little boy, standing perfectly happily beside his cannon. I didn't think anything but death could bring back that look to his face.

HORTENSIA. You are more observant than I, my dear. I thought he seemed a little absent during dinner—nothing more.

COUNTESS. And you allow him to absent himself? I was never Tiger's mistress, but if I had been, I promise you, I'd never have allowed it.

HORTENSIA. Have you ever seen Tiger talk for ten minutes without a stop? He starts a sentence, his voice runs on in exactly the same way; what he's saying is sometimes very amusing —but he isn't there any more. When he has to answer, he sounds like a sleepwalker, a sleepwalker with all his wits about him; then suddenly, the moment you least expect it, he's back.

COUNTESS. Tiger is absentminded and unstable. His mother was exactly the same, but as she had less imagination, she removed her presence bodily. When you called on her, she would leave the room a dozen times in ten minutes, on any pretext. Once I watched her through a bay window—she simply went outside the front door, waited a few moments, and came back again. I've always put up with these little escapings from Tiger. But there are absences and absences. If he goes, he goes; but I insist on knowing with whom he goes. I tell you he loves her, Hortensia!

HORTENSIA. Tiger is incapable of love!

COUNTESS. I tell you, he's in process of learning! You may do as you please; I shall never put up with it. Were things successful with you physically?

HORTENSIA. You embarrass me, Eliane.

COUNTESS. My dear Hortensia, this isn't the time to be prudish. We have to protect ourselves. Was he always very amorous?

HORTENSIA. Tiger is a wonderful lover.

COUNTESS. That's what they all tell me. But after all, there are degrees of success. . . . Tiger catches fire, in an instant, at sight of a supple figure. The only secret of beauty, he insists, is the way a fine bust is borne above a slender waist, with real hips below. I've known him follow gypsies for hours in the street, women reeking of goats and stale tobacco; girls padding along barefoot in the mud, or teetering on impossible heels. He swore they were princesses, the only women who knew how to walk. He's had I don't know how many watches stolen, trying to make friends with such creatures; I can't imagine what miracle kept him from having his throat cut by their pimps ten times over. I tell you this simply to show you how strong his desires are. But I know him. He's not the man to live on aesthetic considerations. And he has too great a horror of bungling not to insist that this game, too, must be played to perfection. Let us put our cards on the table, Hortensia. I must know if I can count on you. Was it successful between the two of you, on that level?

HORTENSIA. Dear Eliane, would you like details?

COUNTESS. Thank you, no. That particular activity of Tiger's concerns me as much as his passion for polo. But, after all, when he comes home from a match, I can ask him quite frankly if his horse disappointed him . . . in his love affairs, I have always stopped at speculation. This time I need to know.

HORTENSIA. I don't think his horse disappoints him.

COUNTESS. Good. That's important. He hasn't touched that child yet. She's a virgin, that sticks out a mile, probably clumsy and without flair. The troubled state of his heart—and there's no doubt about that—may find itself without any real support. If he does make an incursion into the west wing, he may come straight back to us, utterly deflated. He has a morbid horror of failure.

HORTENSIA. Eliane, it's my turn to find your feelings limited. Love, even restricted to that, is an infinitely more subtle game than polo. The heart may very well mingle itself with the pleasures of the flesh in an unexpected fashion. I can only speak by hearsay; but I imagine that a tender feeling for a new little person who gives herself clumsily, might teach Tiger a host of new joys—even beyond desire, or perhaps subtly fused with desire.

COUNTESS. I don't like a woman to understand too well what her lover may feel with another. I thought you more normal, Hortensia. On my own level, where I know I have remained Tiger's wife, the level of intelligence and our mutual tastes in life, I feel instinctively there's a chance he may escape me. That's quite enough. I must act. With or without you.

HORTENSIA. With me, of course. What do you take me for? I'm interested in nothing at the moment but getting Tiger back, even if I leave him next morning.

COUNTESS. Do both, my dear, and I'll be much obliged! In the intervals between two mistresses, Tiger is an entrancing husband. He usually feels the need to take me traveling and pay discreet court to me—all entirely platonic, naturally—but I have never been wildly sensual. I shall profit by the occasion to leave Villebosse, who is beginning to bore me. It will be divine.

HORTENSIA. Eliane, I'm delighted to assist your honeymoon with all the modest means at my disposal! Where will you go—Italy?

COUNTESS. That's very overdone. That's where Tiger took me the first time, when I still believed in the moon. It would remind me of my disappointments. Tiger is dying to go to Japan. He, who yawns his way around the world, tells me it's the only country for which he feels the least curiosity.

HORTENSIA. Japan is a charming country. Let's set to work on your trip to Japan. How shall we go about it?

COUNTESS. Dear little Hortensia! Let me kiss you. (*She does so*) Tell me whether, in your heart of hearts, you care for him so little? You aren't going to play me the dirty trick of leaving him stuck with that child? I have the impression I dropped my guard a little while I was talking to you just now.

HORTENSIA. (*Embracing her*) Dear Eliane! I should be delighted to play you some little mischief of that sort. I shall never forgive you for staying friends with Tiger all the time he has been my lover. But don't worry; my pride is stronger than my feelings. I can't allow him to leave me for that little trollop. I propose to do the leaving myself. I shall reserve my revenge on you for some other time.

COUNTESS. (*Kissing her again*) What a dear it is, and how deliciously it smells! It's still "Plaisir d'Une Nuit," isn't it? I used to think it smelled like Turkish delight. But I've got used to it. So sad that just when I've stopped noticing it, Tiger won't reek of it any more! Come to my room, my love. I have a very simple plan I want to tell you about. That little ninny is bound to be crammed with complexes and wounded pride. I shall say I've been robbed of a trinket —I shall insist on all the servants' rooms being searched, her own included. Afterwards, we'll find the thing no matter where—on one of the garden paths, or under a sofa cushion—that's a mere detail. But it might be enough to drive her away. It's quite extraordinary, my dear, how sensitive the poor can be.

> *They go out. The* COUNT *and* HERO *enter through another door.*

HERO. Do we rehearse or do we not, as Villebosse says? I can just about bear my waistcoat for three acts, not more. Luckily, the classics are short. If you'd insisted on giving one of Victor Hugo's dramas, I should have exploded before the end, scattering my liver like a shower of poisoned flowers over the guests. What a splendid exit for a drunk!

COUNT. (*Sitting down*) Hero, I'm not enjoying it any more.

HERO. You're tired of Marivaux? Thank God for that. All the same you're not asking us to change the play? I was so pleased with my part. A lord! What are you playing, my dear Hero? A lord. It sounded discreet and mysterious, and there weren't too many lines to remember.

COUNT. It doesn't amuse me any more to amuse myself.

HERO. You've taken long enough to find that out.
 He helps himself and offers a glass to the COUNT.
I discovered the remedy twenty years ago. Have a drink.

COUNT. It wouldn't amuse me to get drunk.

HERO. Do you think one gets drunk to amuse oneself? To be a drunkard is no soft option . . . If you knew the care and perseverance it takes . . . Always emptying glasses and filling them up again . . . People take you for a rich idler, when all you are is a bottle washer. I've got an idea. Work.

COUNT. It's a bad habit which must be learned very young. Besides, I don't believe it would amuse me.

HERO. Do as I do, make love. Change your women. It's not so hilarious as it sounds, but it keeps hope alive.

COUNT. I have tried it—less than you, but I've tried. Let me tell you, taking it all in all, I don't believe it's an occupation for a man.

HERO. You're depressing me. How old are you?

COUNT. A year older than you. You've known that since the first grade, when I joined you at school a year late. We owe our friendship to my scarlatina.

HERO. You're not concealing a desire to dedicate your life to a useful purpose?

COUNT. Certainly not. I know what that means, too.

HERO. Nor a sudden passion for making money? With Eliane's fortune it would be quite immoral and in very bad taste.

COUNT. I hate money.

HERO. No big words. Despise it, that's enough. There's only one solution for you—neurasthenia. It's a state of mind. Everything you say will seem profound. And above all, the days will hardly be long enough for the nursing you'll have to give yourself. The doctors have brought back into fashion treatments as old as Adam. There was a time when the Confessional was extremely uncomfortable. Now they stretch you out on a sofa, and make you talk away for a whole hour, every day. It's always enthralling to talk about oneself, it's the one subject one never grows tired of. It'll cost you a fortune, and at the year's end you'll discover that you enjoyed suckling your nurse and your troubles probably resulted from that. You'll have to resign yourself to being cured and think of something else. But at least it'll help you to get through twelve months.

COUNT. Imagine, Hero, that one day everything slipped into place around you. That everything became simple and peaceful, but at the same time, inaccessible.

HERO. I haven't much imagination. Wait while I transpose . . . Alcohol is suddenly prescribed by my doctors as the elixir of life, but at that precise moment, all the bars I know are closed.

COUNT. That's right. No, it's not. There is one bar open, just one. A poor little provincial café where you'd never think of going.

HERO. There's no such thing as a poor little provincial café where I'd never think of going.

COUNT. You go in all the same, by accident, or design, and once over the threshold, you discover that life is vastly more simple, very much more serious—and very much better than you ever thought it could be.

HERO. These analogies dredged up from the drink trade are somewhat obscure and in very doubtful taste. Besides, I'm afraid they're making me thirsty. Enough of parables. You're in love.

COUNT. Yes.

HERO. Good. It can't be serious. You've told me that at least ten times before.

COUNT. So I have. Very well, I am not in love.

HERO. Then it's real? You've told me that at least three times, on two occasions with tears.

COUNT. Very well, have it your own way. This time it isn't real. Because it's like nothing I have ever known.

HERO. (*Gets up, looks at him while he fills his glass and says suddenly, in another voice*) You disgust me.

COUNT. Why?

HERO. (*Gently*) I don't like the way you look.

COUNT. Am I ugly?

HERO. No. You are transfigured. Your face is beautiful again. Not as women see it; as I alone know. You look as you did at Sainte-Barbe when we were fifteen; in the days before we climbed the wall together to visit a brothel. As you did when we came back from football in winter, muddy, sweating and happy, whistling together after the girls. As you did that night in the dormitory when we swore eternal friendship, and hacked at our arms with a rusty penknife, so we could mingle our blood. (*In a low voice*) Don't play me that trick, Tiger, I should never forgive you.

COUNT. It took us an hour to carve ourselves up. What cowards we both were, in spite of our noble exaltation! Yet we did it all the same. Do you remember the vow?

HERO. (*Harshly*) No!

COUNT. I could say it for you. I came across it last night, quite by chance.

HERO. No. I don't want to remember. Don't do this to me, Tiger. Look, my hands are shaking, I'm a miserable wreck, in a year or two at latest they'll either trundle me along in a bath chair, or I'll be dead. I couldn't bear for you to become him again now. It would be only too easy.

COUNT. Whom?

HERO. (*Brutally*) You know!
    He grips the glass in his hand so tightly it breaks.
    They both look at the glass and Hero says gently:
I'm sorry, dear boy. I like to break things.

COUNT. You're mad! You're bleeding. Take my handkerchief. You've been looking on the wine when it's red.

HERO. (*Tying up his hand*) Wine is always red, let me tell you. You should find that out.
    He holds out a piece of glass.
Cut yourself, Tiger, and let us swear an oath.

COUNT. What oath?

HERO. That we're both content with each other as we are, and we'll go on bravely amusing ourselves to the end. If you're tired of Hortensia, take another mistress. If you're short of money, I'll keep you supplied. If you want to forget, I'll teach you how to drink. But enjoy yourself as I do, please. And don't look like that any more.

COUNT. I can't help it. What can I do?

HERO. We all have to choose, Tiger. And we have chosen. It's too late.

He has poured himself another drink, now he changes his tone.

Besides, it would grieve me, dear fellow, to see you make a fool of yourself. . . . And grieve me far more to see you happy in that way.

COUNT. (*After a pause*) You've never forgiven me for Evangéline, have you?

HERO. No.

COUNT. But, my dear boy, it was no kind of marriage for you. You were nineteen. You would have buried yourself, you . . . (*He stops*) Forgive me. Today, for the first time, I see I might have been wrong when I stopped you marrying that girl.

HERO. What's done is done. You weren't wrong. We've had plenty of fun together, since then. No regrets! Between my six children, my wife and my gun dogs, in some little provincial château, I should certainly have come to the same end—somewhat less brilliantly, that's all. In our family, we are families from father to son, just as in other families they're all upholsterers. But one good piece of advice deserves another. Leave what they call love alone. It's not for us.

COUNT. If you love me, you should want me to be happy.

HERO. Not any more. Not like that. Besides, we mustn't either of us cling to our illusions. We haven't loved each other for twenty years—not since we went into long trousers. That doesn't prevent us being good friends.
He pours him a drink.
Let's drink together, Tiger. Amuse yourself how you like. After all, you are free. But no more confidences. Besides, one mustn't hope too much, not any more. Life takes pains to put things in order and keep them that way. Life's an orderly business.

COUNT. We shall see.

HERO. We shall see. One always sees. That's what's so marvelous in the human condition. We cry "Eureka" five minutes before we die, and the curtain falls on that consoling word.
The COUNTESS *has entered with* HORTENSIA.
Good morning, Eliane.

COUNTESS. Good morning, Hero. Tiger, I'm very upset. I must speak to you. My emerald ring has disappeared.

COUNT. Ask your maid to look for it, my dear. Not me—I have a horror of such exercises. You prick your fingers on the sofa cushions, fill your nails with dirt, and disinter an ancient letter, which always makes unpleasant reading—when it isn't a bill.

COUNTESS. We've been searching all the morning. I had it yesterday. In this room. I left it in the cloakroom, where we keep our costumes, because I thought the green didn't go with my dress. I'm very upset. I'm afraid someone may have behaved badly.

COUNT. Now, no nonsense. Look in the cloakroom again.

COUNTESS. Of course. But if I don't find it, I ought to tell the insurance people. They'll send someone down to make inquiries. It will be odious.

COUNT. After the ball, my dear, after the ball. You don't expect me to clap your minions of the law into Louis Quatorze costumes, hoping nobody will notice them? After the ball, please.

COUNTESS. I'm sorry, Tiger, but the insurance people must be notified within twenty-four hours. I shall go and search again. Will you help me, Hero?

HERO. Delighted to be of use! It must be my first chance for thirty-seven years.

COUNT. (*Calling to her as she goes out with* HERO) But no fuss, I implore you! (*To* HORTENSIA) My dear, one's whole life is poisoned by fear of burglars and shipwrecks and if, in fact, you question the people around you, no one has ever been robbed and the ship has never gone down. Haven't you noticed that curious fact—life, real life, with murders, ferocious passions, cataclysms, fabulous inheritance, takes place almost exclusively in the newspapers? Of course, in wartime you may accidentally find your activities featured in a communiqué; even so, war's only impressive because it makes so much noise. When all's said and done, I'm sure it's the disease that kills the fewest people.

HORTENSIA. This ring business is most annoying.

COUNT. Of course it's annoying. But Eliane has so many jewels, she can afford to lose one now and again. After all, it would be immoral if it was always the same women who wore them.

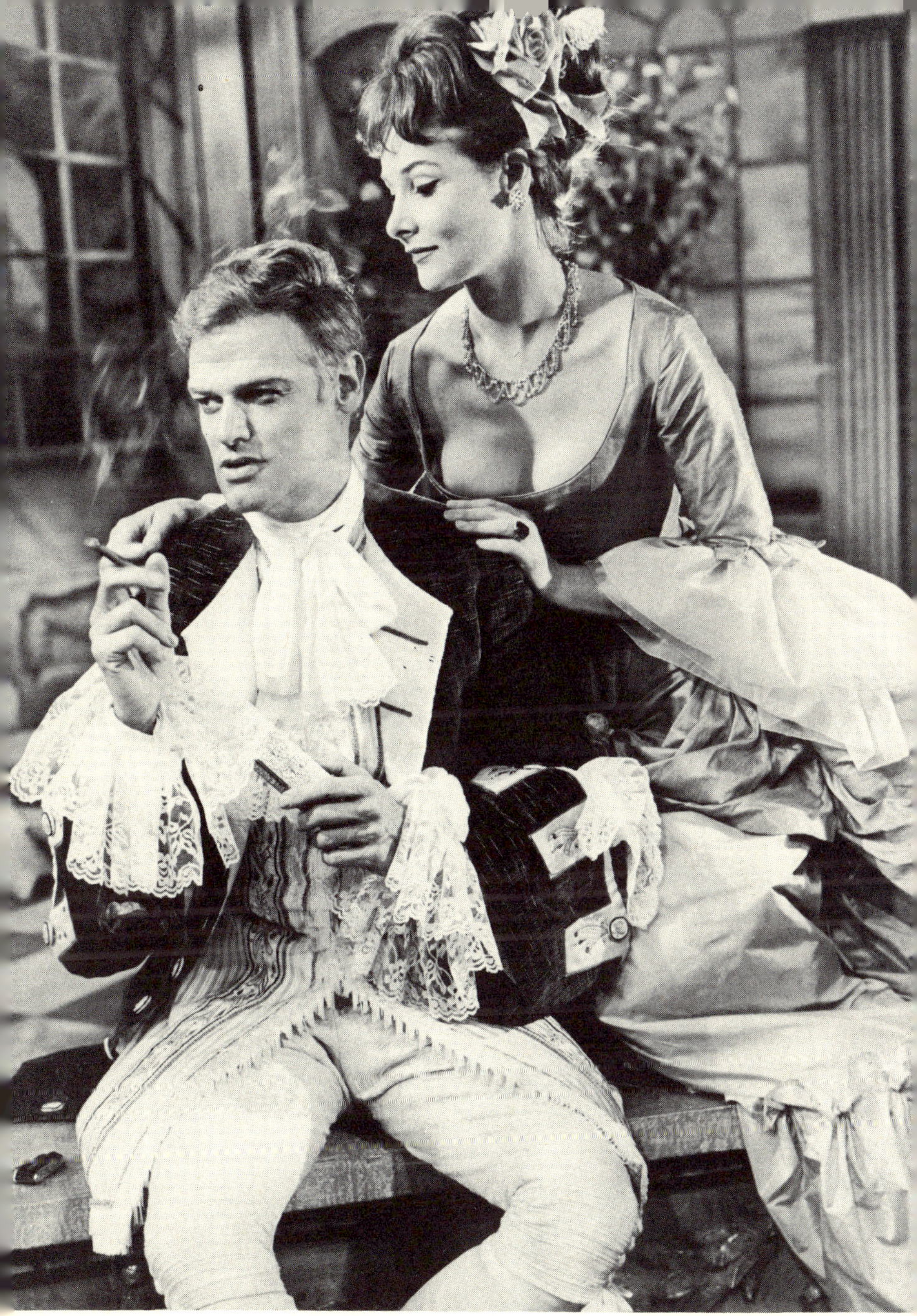

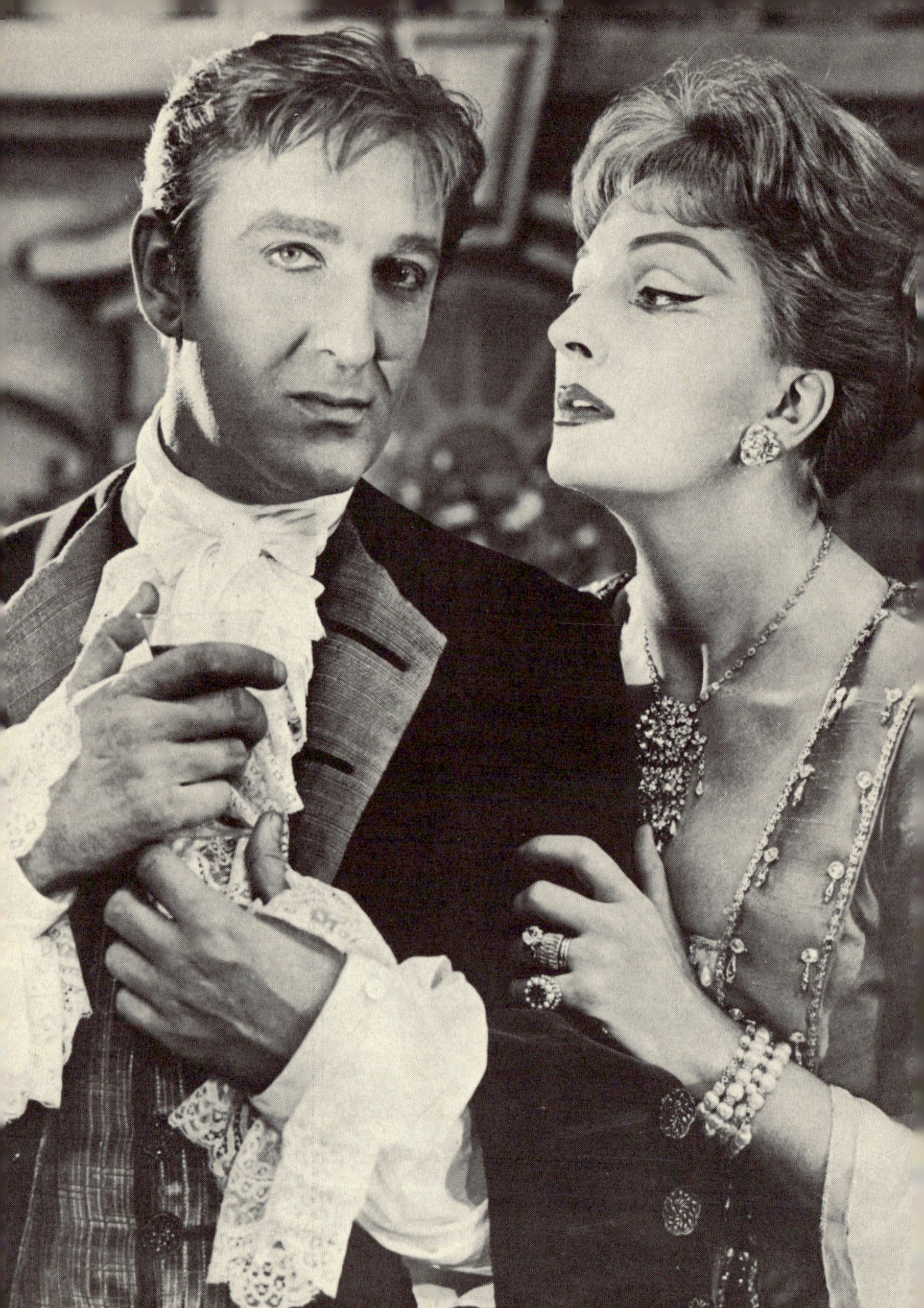

HORTENSIA. I'm sure Eliane is taking it less cheerfully. It was an admirable stone. She means to search all the servants' rooms.

COUNT. Every one of them has been with the family for twenty years. Surely, if they were going to steal from her they'd have done it already. Her own maid's younger, of course, but then she's her goddaughter: the child was littered in the kitchen, like the kittens. Besides, she spends her entire time going to Mass. Unless she wanted to buy candles, I really don't see why the trinket should interest her.

HORTENSIA. Well, Eliane has decided to search the whole house. It seems the most elementary precaution. Now, who else is here, besides the servants? . . . Villebosse, Hero, Monsieur Damiens, me . . .

COUNT. (*Interrupting*) My dear, I abominate detective stories. I think they're the most ridiculous things on earth. Torturing oneself to cook up a complicated story, merely to give a bogus elegance to three pages of denouement at the end, is a fool's game. If I ever happen to open one in bed, after a discouraging evening, I always drop off to sleep before the villain is unmasked. And I'm never interested enough to open the book again next morning. There are a whole series of dark crimes of that order whose authors I shall never know. I can bear the loss with equanimity. One oughtn't to look for criminals in real life, either. It's the most futile game in the world. Either everyone's guilty, or nobody's to blame.

HORTENSIA. Your taste for paradox threatens to lead you astray, Tiger. I don't think Eliane's is as developed as yours. If I know anything about her, she'll have all the rooms in the west wing searched, as she said she would.

COUNT. (*A little sharply*) If Eliane has the west wing searched, I insist that the east wing be searched as well. I shall lose my watch, my dear, and hide it in your bedroom! (*He looks at her, hard*) Did you think up this little story together? I congratulate you.

HORTENSIA. (*Suddenly very innocent*) What story, Tiger?

COUNT. (*Draws her to her feet, says squarely*) My dear Hortensia, I loved you once. It's too grand a word, of course, but we have so few that we must group a good many sentiments under the same heading. My hands, in any case, have loved you. Every time we met, I knew a sort of joy, very pure—yes, it's strange, very pure—and very close to happiness in touching you.

HORTENSIA. Thank you, Tiger.

COUNT. Don't thank me. It has nothing to do with you. I'm going to pay you a compliment, Hortensia, the first and probably the last—you're very beautiful. I don't mean your face; that is charming, of course, but I don't much believe in faces. Besides, with the universal fashion for cosmetics, all women who aren't positively ugly look alike. But your body is very beautiful, noble and beautiful like an animal's. And in true beauty there is always something solemn. If God exists, such beauty must reflect a little of Himself.

HORTENSIA. Good God!

COUNT. Yes. An odd word in my mouth. Believe me, I'm quite conscious of sounding absurd when I say it. But the memory of the day I held you in my arms for the first time is as clear and dazzling as a memory of my childhood: the first palace my father showed me in Italy. The same stab of pain and the same joy. Eliane's a woman of intellect, but

I rate that low; it's the weapon of the poor. Let intellect play her ugly little game alone—haggle like a fishwife; as for you, stay out of it. Be worthy of your beauty. Beauty's a great lady.

HORTENSIA. This must be a new game, Tiger, you don't usually talk so gravely. You're scaring me.

COUNT. (*Letting her go and lighting a cigar*) I'm scaring myself, a little. Do you believe it amuses me to navigate such deep waters? I'm not used to it. Any minute now, I expect to start gasping for air.

HORTENSIA. Tiger, that child isn't even pretty. She's shrewd and docile, but she doesn't even know how to behave. She will shame you by her little nursemaid's frock, the first time you take her out, and if you try to dress her up, she'll shame you even more. I know you.

COUNT. I'm stupid enough to feel ashamed, it's true. But that has nothing to do with it.

HORTENSIA. You belong to a different world, Tiger. The head and the heart commit a thousand follies, the hands are rarely mistaken. I'm sure you still want me.

COUNT. (*Looks at her smilingly and says gently*) Of course I do. I'm capable of anything. Only, you see, I love her.

HORTENSIA. Really, Tiger, it's absurd! She's the opposite of everything you could love.

COUNT. The opposite. Exactly. And I love her. That's comic, don't you think?

HORTENSIA. (*Turning away, bursting out laughing*) Oh, it's too stupid! It's really too stupid! Forgive me, but I assure you, it's too stupid!

COUNT. Yes, it is stupid. This adventure is making me wholly stupid. But it's delicious. I couldn't bear never to have felt like this.

M. DAMIENS. (*Entering*) Monsieur le Comte, Madame la Comtesse has just discovered the loss of a ring. She has ordered her butler and steward to search the bedrooms in the west wing. Just now, you gave me assurance of the respect you intended to have shown to my goddaughter in this house. Will you allow her room to be searched?

COUNT. Certainly not, Damiens. Come with me. We'll put an end to this charade.
They go out. VILLEBOSSE *enters.*

VILLEBOSSE. Once and for all, do we rehearse or do we not? We've been dressed for the last two hours.

HORTENSIA. But we're all acting, Villebosse! We're in the thick of a comedy. Haven't you noticed it yet?
She sweeps out.

VILLEBOSSE. I swear they're all laughing at me.
To HERO, *who enters:*
Sir!

HERO. Sir?

VILLEBOSSE. Everyone in this house is laughing at me!

HERO. It's quite possible.

VILLEBOSSE. Sir, I have the impression that you're at the bottom of this distasteful behavior.

HERO. That's equally possible, sir.

VILLEBOSSE. What would you say, sir, if I insisted on reparation?

THE REHEARSAL

HERO. Sir, I love to break, but I never repair.
He goes out.

VILLEBOSSE. (*Shouting after him*) Sir, you have refused my challenge! I shall publish it everywhere! I'll cover you with shame!

COUNTESS. (*Entering, beside herself*) Villebosse!

VILLEBOSSE. Eliane, my love.

COUNTESS. Tiger has just insulted me unbearably. One of my jewels has been stolen. When I told the servants to search the rooms in the west wing, Tiger forbade them to enter the room of that brat he's forced on us all for the last week. He's sworn that if they search her room, they must search mine first. He claims that I haven't lost the ring, but hidden it. It's insulting! His behavior's been utterly caddish.

VILLEBOSSE. I won't tolerate it, Eliane! Allow me to challenge him!

COUNTESS. Villebosse! Will you never understand anything? Are you trying to madden me further? There's no question of challenging Tiger because he's failed in respect for me. It's his right—I am his wife! It's a question of impressing on him that he's making a fool of me by flaunting himself with that little nobody of a nursemaid. After all, Villebosse, he must have his mistresses! Hortensia is my friend, and she is quite impeccable. But what will people say if my husband loses his head over a guttersnipe? If he takes her back to Paris, Villebosse, I'll be unable to leave my house the whole winter. Positively, I shan't dare to show my face again.

VILLEBOSSE. It's intolerable! I shall settle everything. Count on me, Eliane!
He goes out. LUCILE *enters.*

LUCILE. I have brought you the key of my room, madame. I want it to be searched with all the others. Besides, they may well find the jewel there, and then everyone will feel better.

COUNTESS. I don't know what you mean, my child. My maid is still searching my own room and my husband is helping her. It is, of course, quite possible that I have put the ring away somewhere and forgotten about it.

LUCILE. That would be good news.

COUNTESS. Yes. Suspicions are always horrid for everyone. I'm sorry if I've hurt your feelings. It was merely a general measure that concerned the whole staff. I expect you've come to tell me you want to give up your part in the play. Perhaps you don't even want to go on looking after the children? The poor little souls had grown so fond of you already, everyone tells me. Do think it over. I'm sure it will break their hearts. But still, if your decision is unshakable, I think the best thing would be to act as quickly and as brutally as possible. With children, as I don't have to tell you, one has to be very clear-cut. They'll cry their eyes out all night long, but next morning they'll have forgotten all about it and begin to love somebody else. I believe there's a train in an hour's time. The car can take you to the station as soon as your bag is packed. Naturally—although the decision is yours—I shall pay you for six months' wages. I know how awkwardly you're placed.

> *The* COUNT *has entered. The* COUNTESS *turns to him, very much at ease.*

Mademoiselle tells me she's leaving us. I'm terribly sorry about your play, Tiger, but in three days we can easily replace her. I told her that so far as the children were concerned, if she'd really made up her mind, it would be much better to go away at once, without seeing them again. They're immensely attached to her already, as we all are, but we mustn't risk having them make an even worse fuss later on.

COUNT. Here is your emerald, Eliane.

COUNTESS. (*Putting it on her finger*) Oh, how splendid. Where was it?

COUNT. In your own room. Under one of the candlesticks.

COUNTESS. Heavens! Why on earth should I have put it there?

COUNT. Now I must ask you to apologize to Mademoiselle.

COUNTESS. Apologize? What for? But of course, with all my heart. . . . I am distressed at my stupidity, mademoiselle. I hope you'll forgive me and not carry away too unhappy a memory of this house. I am sure you will agree, Tiger, that Fourcault should give the child six months' wages. I know it's merely impulsiveness on her part, but after all, if I hadn't mislaid my ring, she wouldn't have thought of leaving us.

COUNT. My dear Eliane, you know I never allow the smallest inconvenience to interfere with an entertainment once I've decided to give it. We can neither cancel the performance nor recast the part in three days. Please be good enough to see that Mademoiselle retracts her decision.

COUNTESS. Indeed, I've said all I could, Tiger. Her feelings are hurt. She insists on going. And I must admit I understand how she feels.

COUNT. I'm sure there's still something you can say. I count on this small diplomatic success on your part, Eliane, or you'll disappoint me exceedingly. I'll leave you together. In half an hour's time, we rehearse.

He has gone. LUCILE *still says nothing. The* COUNTESS *sits down, very much at ease.*

COUNTESS. There now! It seems I must induce you to stay, under pain of quarreling with Tiger to the death. You must admit it's funny! But I'm a weak creature, and Tiger's whims are my Holy Writ. You're still very young. . . . When the times comes to choose, mademoiselle, never fall in love with a frivolous man.

LUCILE. (*Gently*) Are you in love with him?

COUNTESS. What a question, mademoiselle! He's my husband.

LUCILE. Do you think he can be happy amusing himself all the time?

COUNTESS. My dear child, don't expect me to allow our interview—since apparently we must have one—to take on that tone. I have a horror of familiarities. When I was a child, we had an English governess who taught me never to ask personal questions. Since it is your profession to educate children, try to teach them very early in life that nothing is more ill-mannered. Tiger has begged me to ask you to stay. I am asking you. If he has to cancel this performance, he will make himself ill. Besides, why should you go? We very much appreciate your services to our little unfortunates, and so far as we're concerned, we certainly shan't prolong our own stay at Ferbroques. Tiger is bored to death in the country. As soon as the entertainment's over, we shall return to Paris, for the season. So everything will slip back into place, isn't that so? Let us part good friends, and once more, forgive me for this little incident. Tiger would be capable of sulking with me for a whole week if he felt you were still vexed with me. You and I know very little of each other; but you appreciate the respect I have for your godfather, Monsieur Damiens. I was talking about you to him this morning. Now there's a man who's extremely fond of you.

LUCILE. Yes. So he tells me.

COUNTESS. He has suffered a great deal too, I believe. He's been separated from his wife for years, hasn't he? And even during their life together, she doesn't seem to have brought him the comfort he might have expected. He quite astonishes one by the sensibility hidden under that rather stern exterior. He talked to me about you at great length.

LUCILE. Really?

COUNTESS. Yes. My dear child, I lost my temper a little too quickly, I admit. As Tiger tells me every day, women are quite mad—just for a touch of foolish jealousy, they will compromise in a single moment all the esteem their virtues have won them in ten years. You know, I like you a great deal. . . . You're really so young, so defenseless with your little air of knowing everything. I'm sure that under all that high-mindedness, you're more than ready to burn your wings like a delicate insect at the first candle that comes your way. You say to yourself, won't it be beautiful! At last it will be the life I've always dreamed about. For a week you live in that dream, and afterwards, you're left with only your eyes to weep with. Damiens told me you were proud and poor. That's a great virtue, with a very great defect. Of course, you may well meet an excellent young man in your own milieu. But that won't last long either, believe me. The charming squire of the country dances, the young man, all blushes, who picks flowers for you at Meudon, it won't be more than a couple of years before he turns into a sulky, bad-tempered little tyrant, who gives you nothing but his socks to mend and sits every evening in his shirt sleeves, with his nose buried in the newspaper. You're worth something better than forced labor in the household, with an ugly little brat, the spit of his father, dragging at your skirts. To be reckless is a great temptation; to be wise is a temptation also—sometimes as dangerous as the others. When a girl's fastidious, pretty, clever and penniless, she's always a little déclassée. You must make your choice. Damiens—who is my friend—and I, were very worried about you this morning.

>*Pause. She rises. She waves negligently toward a little worktable.*

After all, his wife's a thousand miles away, in the country; she's ill, she's older than he is, she can't live forever. Damiens is a man of honor, and still very good-looking. I remember him, fifteen or twenty years ago, when he came to my mother's house—shall I tell you, my dear? I was in love with him a whole winter—of course, I was a child then. . . . Still, think it over. I can speak to you as a woman who knows what life is, who is very much older than you are, and who would be miserable—really miserable—to see you ruining your beautiful youth for some folly with no future to it. When one has no real standing, like yourself, and is alone in the world, one's first thought must be for the future. Heavens! I know it can't be much fun—at twenty, one has all sorts of other dreams—but that's the way the world goes, my dear. We can do nothing about it.

>*Pause. She looks at* LUCILE *and says suddenly:*

Damiens has served us long and faithfully. May I say, that in my eyes it would be as if you had become his wife? In

THE REHEARSAL

fact, this very emerald would be my wedding present. (*She holds out the ring*)

LUCILE. (*Looks at the ring for an instant, then hands it back*) It's too beautiful a present for that kind of ceremony. No, thank you, madame.

COUNTESS. (*Taking back the ring*) You're making a mistake. It was sincerely meant.

LUCILE. Besides, whether in that way or another, I know I shall never marry. I have sworn it.

COUNTESS. How can you know, at your age? How long ago did you make that bold decision?

LUCILE. (*Gently*) Last night.

COUNTESS. (*Rising suddenly*) Very well. When you see Tiger again, I shall be obliged if you'll tell him that I did all I could.

LUCILE. I'll tell him. Thank you, madame.

> *She goes out. The* COUNTESS *takes a few nervous steps, using her fan as if she were really acting in a play by Marivaux. Then she opens the window and calls.*

COUNTESS. Hero! No, not you, Villebosse! Hero. Come up here at once. I want to speak to you.

> *A moment of silence, several more nervous steps, more playing with the fan, and* HERO *appears.*

HERO. We must stop Tiger making a fool of himself. He loves that child. She's been his mistress since last night and she's told him she loves him. It's ludicrous and it's mad. I don't know if you've noticed him this last week . . . ?

HERO. (*Impassive, glass in hand*) Oh yes, I've noticed.

COUNTESS. It's revolting.

HERO. Revolting. So I told him.

COUNTESS. Are you on my side, Hero? Then do something. Only you can do something, I'm sure of that.

HERO. Do something with him? Tiger is impenetrably kind . . .

COUNTESS. With her, perhaps.

HERO. (*Declaiming*) "And what commandment do you lay upon me? To please that woman and become her lover?"

COUNTESS. You can, Hero, if you put your mind to it. The child's a crazy romantic, no better than a shopgirl, maybe worse. Everyone knows you're irresistible. Seduce her. Never mind if we're acting *Ruy Blas*. After all, we adored it in our teens.

HERO. There's only one difficulty. This girl isn't everyone. She doesn't know I'm irresistible. That cuts out half my chances.

COUNTESS. Nonsense! In two days' time, you and Tiger will become confused in her mind. She'll burst with satisfaction, like any other girl, when the two most brilliant men of the party pay attention to no one but her. I know these little Puritans! I was like that myself before Tiger married me. Women are women, my dear, always, even when they give themselves the airs of angels. I don't have to tell you what to do, my dear Hero. Give her a few drinks one evening, swear you love her. Add a little moonlight and music, and the little ninny will believe you. At least, she'll believe you enough to surrender herself for one night. Afterwards, Tiger will throw her over, or if he agrees to share her, the real danger will be over.

HERO. You're doing me a great honor, Eliane, in being so certain no one can resist me. I'd say yes, for any grown woman, even if she didn't know what everyone knows. After all, I'm a professional! But an innocent young girl—oh no. They're very strange creatures, and I haven't had much to do with them.

COUNTESS. I tell you she's no longer innocent! She's his mistress!

HERO. Since last night. She'll keep her state of grace a little longer.

COUNTESS. Then you'll allow Tiger to make a complete fool of himself? Swamp himself in ridicule? He loves her, Hero, he loves her, I'm sure of it. Don't you care whether he's in love, just like an adolescent boy?

HERO. (*Suddenly very hard*) You're wrong. I do care.

COUNTESS. Are you afraid of hurting him? Of breaking both their hearts?

HERO. It's not that either. I told you: I like breaking things.
A silence.

COUNTESS. (*Going to him*) Hero, she sleeps alone, at the end of the west wing. It isn't certain you could seduce her, assuming she really loves him. And if he loves her too, Tiger might intervene, carry her away. But we all know you're a brute. You're mad for the child . . . as usual, you've been drinking. You force her door, I'll see that the lock's out of order. Of course she'll cry for help, but she's miles out of earshot there, and besides, what can a young girl do with her nails, her feeble fists, her tears, against the desires of a grown man? If she loves him she'll run away next morning, out of pure shame.

HERO. (*Another silence. Then he says softly*) Evangéline!

COUNTESS. What was that?

HERO. The name of a young girl. You must have met her. She married a banker, a Mr. Blumenstein. She was very beautiful. Her marriage was unhappy and she died many years ago.

COUNTESS. A slim young thing, fair, with wonderful great eyes? Like a sacrificial fawn? I remember her very well. She was presented to me at the Rothschilds'. But where's the connection?

HERO. Very slight and very far away. I'm glad you remember her. . . . Come on, Eliane, let's go and rehearse; they're waiting for us, and this play has got to be well acted, no matter what happens. Like all trifles, it's immensely important. Her husband was a swine. It was even said that he beat her . . .

COUNTESS. (*Going*) I've had an idea. I shall arrange for a telegram to be sent to Tiger, calling him away this evening. . . . Gontaut-Biron will see to it for me.

They have gone.

CURTAIN

Act Three

SCENE ONE

> A small attic room. LUCILE, in a dressing gown, is lying on the bed, reading. The door opens softly. She looks up, surprised. It is HERO, still in costume, his jabot slightly awry, a bottle and two glasses in his arms. She sits up.

HERO. (*Smiling*) Don't be afraid. Tiger's just telephoned to say he won't be back till late tonight. He asked me to give you the message and keep you company for a while.
> LUCILE *has risen, surprised. He enters.*
May I sit down?

LUCILE. (*Pointing to the only chair*) Yes.

HERO. (*Sitting down*) How very odd, when there are so many useless chairs in this château! I suppose they didn't cater for visitors in the west wing. You take the bed, my angel, you'll be more comfortable. . . . Have a little drink?

LUCILE. No.

HERO. Your mistake! You don't mind if I help myself? In my present state, it would be unwise of me to stop. I should be drunk in a flash and behave very badly. If I drink a little more, I postpone the hour of reckoning. . . . You won't be bored if I chat with you for a little? When the others sleep, I begin my long solitary struggle till dawn, when at last I can shut one eye. Damn that eye! There it is, open wide again, taking in everything. Everything bores it stiff, too, but it goes on staring, stubborn little devil! Even if I'm dying for sleep, even if I've been wide awake for twenty-four hours. In the daytime, I can manage all right. I drink a little, I talk a little—never mind what I talk about. The sound of my own voice keeps me from thinking. But when the rest of you are all safely in bed, then I do start to think, and that's horrible. Would you be good enough to stop me thinking a little? Besides, it's Tiger's express orders. He told me: "Go up and tell her I shan't be coming home and keep her company for a bit."

A silence. He adds, smiling:

He must have hoped you'd speak to me from time to time.

LUCILE. What would you like me to say?

HERO. How should I know? Something pleasant. That you're mistaken; that it isn't Tiger you're in love with, but me . . .

LUCILE *doesn't reply, smiling, huddled on her bed.*

Then tell me you love Tiger . . . it won't be such pleasant hearing, of course, but better than nothing, all the same.

LUCILE. I can't believe he wanted us to talk of that. I can't believe he has discussed me with you.

HERO. Ah, my child! You don't know men. Inveterate gossips. We tell each other everything.

LUCILE. Are you very fond of him?

HERO. We were throwing stink bombs at girls before you dreamed of entering the world, dear baby. We even mingled our blood one night in the dormitory. For life and for death! The occasion of dying for each other didn't present itself immediately, that's all. . . . And since then, we've had to live. Castor and Pollux, you know, that's only a legend. . . . At all events, we're very fond of each other and none of the women in our lives has managed to come between us.

LUCILE. (*Asking like a child*) Has he had lots of women?

HERO. (*Smiling*) Dear baby! He adores you, of course, and with you he's found something he'd completely overlooked; but you must admit it would have been a most unwise gamble on his part to have waited for you. Does it hurt you very much, to think he's had other women?

LUCILE. That's my secret.

HERO. Keep it, my precious, with your little handkerchief tucked in on top! Personally, I'm not much interested in confidences. They're always more or less the same, and only comfort the one who does the confessing. You are young, you're on your voyage to Cythera; you must feel like an explorer, a discoverer of new continents. . . . Don't protest—it's very charming. . . . You'll learn quickly enough that the play has only two or three parts, two or three situations eternally repeated—and that what springs irresistibly from the heart in the greatest moments of ecstasy is never more than a stale platitude, chewed over since the dawn of the world by mouths that in our time have lost all their teeth. There's nothing new to invent. And that includes our vices which are revoltingly precise and commonplace. A whole catalogue, with the market price in the right-hand column. For everything has to be paid for, of course. Sodomy—loneliness and an indiscreet ulcer. Alcoholism—gout and cirrhosis of the liver. Drug taking—police courts and a high tax on one's pleasure. Passion—fatigue. True love—a dear little broken heart. And no discount for cash.

LUCILE. (*Gently, looking at him squarely*) I've loved Tiger since yesterday, and I'm twenty. So your little lecture is a waste of my time.

HERO. (*Bowing*) *Touché!* Congratulations. I see you have forgotten to be stupid. There was only one answer you could give to my drunkard's disenchantment, and you found it at once. What a lucky fellow Tiger is! He's brought this off as well. He succeeds in everything, whether it's horse racing or love.

LUCILE. He's succeeded in what?

HERO. In finding you. In touching you. I must confess that when I came into this room just now, like everyone else in this house, I still took you for one of those little shopgirls who writes to the agony columns, who's had a tiff with her sweetheart. I got myself snubbed. Splendid. That'll teach me to look at girls a little more closely in future. Now we can meet on equal terms and gossip away like old friends. You know, it was a stroke of genius to make everyone take you for an insignificant little mouse.

LUCILE. I am an insignificant little mouse and I can't string three words together. I don't know how he managed to make me talk at all.

HERO. Tiger is good at everything. I'll bet you were a virgin before?

LUCILE *does not reply.*

Here we go! I've hurt her feelings! Are we friends or aren't we? Do have just one glass with me. If I'm the only one drinking, we'll never get down to conversation.

LUCILE. No thank you, sir.

HERO. (*Repeats, laughing*) No thank you, sir! Polite, too. Neat as a new pin. A fine little pebble, all bright and shiny, that Monsieur found on the beach, without even looking for it, swinging along with his hands in his pockets and his nose in the air, as always. I tell you, he has too much luck, it's maddening.

> *His tone surprises* LUCILE *a little. He corrects himself.*

It really is, you know; or anyway, it would madden me if I didn't happen to be so fond of him. But he'll find out that I do love him—not, of course, in the same way as you do— but very much, all the same, and that I can forgive him anything. Let's talk about him, shall we? It will be pleasant and perhaps I shall go to sleep later on. Sure you won't have a drop? No? Well, never mind. It's not often you find two people meeting over a drink to discuss a third whom they both love. That means a lot of love in this sordid world. What made you give yourself to him, all at once like that, for the very first time? After all, you didn't even know him yesterday?

> LUCILE *does not reply.*

I don't pry into secrets. All the same, it must have been so delightful—all of a sudden! It's something so far outside my own experience, it might even convert me. No? You don't want to tell me about it? I'll never know then, even by hearsay, how love is set in motion?

LUCILE. (*Softly, as if to herself, after a pause*) I could never bear anyone to touch me. And yet, when he took me in his arms, I felt I had come to the end of a journey. That's all. I wasn't that poor little girl any more, eternally pushed about from place to place, clutching her bag and being afraid of everything. . . . I had something of my own, at last. What more could you expect me to want? It was an undreamed-of situation to be in!

HERO. Suppose he'd only wanted to amuse himself with you?

LUCILE. That's a risk all girls have to run, something they must find out for themselves. One mustn't get too sentimental over the silly ones.

HERO. All the same, I know the habits of the animal, when it wants to be loved. Didn't he do almost too much to make himself interesting?

LUCILE. (*Smiles, for the first time in agreement with him*) A little too much, yes. But I knew what he meant.

HERO. What could you have hoped for, the first time you set eyes on that jester, that noble mountebank?

LUCILE. No more than to be happy in his arms for a moment, as I was, right away. . . .

HERO. And after that?

LUCILE. After that, if one has to live in the other world, the real world, it's just a matter of earning one's living. . . . There's never any lack of orphans, and nursemaids will always be needed to look after them. That doesn't matter. I should have had my moment.

HERO. (*Lifting his hands*) Not even a clinging vine! Good old Tiger, he manages to escape everything in the world that's in bad taste. He arrives at the height of the party: weariness, futility, sickness of soul. Milord lifts a finger, and behold! An angel appears, who gives herself to him at once and forever. For with you it is forever, isn't it?

LUCILE. Oh yes.

HERO. Oh yes, and if he kills himself in a car crash on his way home tonight, you'll die some time tomorrow? Just taking time to make your little dispositions. Daphnis and Chloe, Dido and Aeneas, Cadmus and Hermione—let's see, what else? Tristram and Iseult without even King Mark and that inconvenient sword between you. One day, Milord feels the time is ripe for an idyl. An idyl? Why, here it is, Monsieur le Comte, on a plate! It's all yours. You had only to express the wish. A young girl, hidden from the common gaze, reticent, a garden enclosed, cultivated with care for you alone? She is here. She is waiting.

LUCILE. That's quite true. I was waiting . . .

HERO. All he had to do was appear! And the idyl is guaranteed spotless and eternal! Let others be content with women who lend themselves to everyone all day before giving themselves to you at night; those women smiling eternally in the shop window like hairdressers' dummies, who live only for pleasure. . . . For I'm sure you'll never learn that trick, you'll always be as prickly, even when he's bought you a whole wardrobe of new dresses and everyone's telling you how pretty you are.

LUCILE. He will never buy me dresses, don't you think it.

HERO. Why not?

LUCILE. Because I won't let him. I've acquired the good habit of buying one myself from time to time, and I shan't change it.

HERO. Everything! Everything! He will have everything. Intelligence, virtue, and altruism thrown in. You are rich; I am poor and proud. Your money might come between us. With a wave of my hand I abolish it. It doesn't exist! Milord needn't even be embarrassed. I bet you'll insist on staying here to look after his aunt's orphans, like a good girl, and content yourself with leaving your door on the latch for him at night.

LUCILE. No, I couldn't do that. But I shall find another children's home near Paris, and he will come and see me whenever he likes.

HERO. That will be nice! He'll ask politely to see you in the parlor and you'll both shake in your shoes when the matron gives you a lecture. He'll blush like a little boy. He'll start wooing you all over again! But there's a slight snag; you don't know our Monsieur. He'll roar like a lion at the mere thought of it. He's a typical French gentleman, with centuries of breeding behind him. He'll never agree to let you go on working.

LUCILE. He will have to. Weren't either of you taught, when you were young, that man must earn his bread by the sweat of his brow?

HERO. No. We went to very distinguished schools, where that formed no part of the curriculum. If they ordered you about, spoke to you rudely, made you watch the clock, Tiger would die of shame, my dear, just that! I know him!

LUCILE. Nobody dies of shame so easily, believe me. Besides, it's not so unpleasant to work—not much more unpleasant than doing nothing, and it takes much less imagination.

When one sees all the trouble you two have to take, just to kill time!

HERO. That's true. We've sweated at it all our lives, both of us. What courage and ambition we must have had, to stick it out! Look at the poor, on Sunday, see what they do with their time. They drag around the streets, they yawn, they're worn out trying to exist until Monday. We've had them seven days a week, those Sundays! Ever since we were children! It hasn't been easy for us. But we have held firm. Now the hardest part is over. Tiger is a man who manages to amuse himself twelve or fifteen hours a day without fatigue. Learn how to do it yourself. He will teach you.

LUCILE. No.

HERO. But if you spend your life in a children's home, while he's at the races, it will be like the daily woman who married a night watchman. You'll never manage to meet. You must be sensible, damn it!

LUCILE. I don't want to be sensible. That's the first word one uses when one is going to do something wicked.

HERO. Something wicked? Something "wicked"? It's a word no one quite knows how to define. In any case, my love, there is something worse, which is to do something stupid.

LUCILE. I want to be stupid! That's my own way of loving. Can you see me installed in a luxurious apartment, for which he pays the rent, and him coming to see me with a little parcel dangling on a ribbon? I should hate him at the end of a week! That would be *really* stupid!

HERO. Little Socrates!

LUCILE. Why little Socrates?

HERO. Because you know all the answers. You're going to stop him making a horrible blunder, and he'll accept it joyfully, the hypocrite. Only too delighted to play the little game! He'll buy himself a nice little suit at the Samaritaine and come and wait for you outside your orphanage at six o'clock with a tuppenny bunch of violets. He'll be twenty again, with all the freshness of youth and all his future before him. To be offered that at forty, just when you start to think you're finished . . .
He rises, and cries out.
Oh no, it's too much! I tell you, it's too much!

LUCILE. Whatever is the matter with you?

HERO. (*Controlling himself, he explains calmly, with a malicious smile*) I'm saying it's too good to be true, that's all. A typical fairy tale.
A silence. They look at each other.

LUCILE. (*Rising*) Sir, we've talked for a little while as he wanted us to do. But now it would be kinder of you, perhaps, to let me go to sleep. I have to get up early in the morning for the children.

HERO. (*Not moving*) We haven't talked for five minutes yet. Do sit down, my love, give me a little while longer. In any case, I shall get less sleep than you will. You can see I'm at a loose end, that I shall die of misery all by myself! Won't you take pity on me, mademoiselle?
LUCILE sits down again on the edge of the bed. He pours himself a drink.
Besides, there's nothing compromising about me. A girl can allow me in her bedroom without danger quite late at

night. Not very appetizing either, I know. A wreck. And I'm a year younger than Tiger. So much for the life of pleasure!

LUCILE. (*Gently*) Why don't you try and drink less?

HERO. Why should I try? I should have to be lucky like Milord and meet an angel who would take me under her wing. Angels are rare!

LUCILE. (*Gently*) Perhaps you'll meet one, some day.

HERO. (*Laughing*) A soak like me? With my drunkard's face, my drunkard's smell? Speaking as an angel, do admit that if I'd been the one to court you, you might have deferred my conversion to a later date?
    He looks at her, smiling.
Another indiscreet question! I'm a bit heavy-handed, I fear. However . . . When you set foot in this house a few days ago, that very first evening at dinner, there wasn't a single man—I except Villebosse, who doesn't count—who looked at anyone but you. That means something, all the same.

LUCILE. (*A little astonished*) All the men?

HERO. Isn't she sweet? She didn't even notice. Yes, my dear, there were three of us. . . . The butler's too old, but Tiger's footman got all the forks mixed up when he was waiting at table. Now there's a lad who was burning to be converted, like the rest of us. Plain as a pikestaff.

LUCILE. Please—that's enough.

HERO. Why? Have I hurt your feelings? Have you still got old-fashioned class prejudices, my love? The boy sleeps in the west wing, too; if I were you, I'd lock and bolt my door at night. We all know he's the son of the grandfather's first footman, but still, he was a paratrooper in the war, and that's an adventure that shook new ideas into people like him. What would you have done had it been he—or perhaps myself—instead of Tiger, who said: I want you?

LUCILE. (*Radiant*) But sir, Tiger's the one I love!

HERO. (*After a pause*) You take the wind out of one's sails. What else can I suggest?

LUCILE. (*Gently*) Nothing.

HERO. Shall we play at let's pretend? Just for a moment or two? Just a little game to kill this long evening that frightens me so much? Now: Tiger hasn't said a word to you; you don't love Tiger. For a week I've watched you quietly, through every meal, and tonight I've made an excuse to come to your room and tell you, as he did, that I want you.

He has got up heavily as he speaks. LUCILE *has also got up.*

LUCILE. That's a game I refuse to play. It would be dreadful. Why can't you understand? You are his friend. If he found out that this was the way you were spending the evening, what would he think?

HERO. You ought to know we've exchanged quite a few mistresses, Tiger and I, as all good friends do. Besides, it would only be tit for tat. . . . There has been an angel in my life, mademoiselle; I was lying to you. A very long time ago. I was nineteen and in those days I hadn't taken to the bottle.

LUCILE. (*Stammering*) And he . . .

HERO. No. He didn't steal her. But he made me leave her for reasons which seemed to me valid enough at the time. She married someone else, who made her miserable, and now she's dead. And it was that brief episode, that short broken engagement, which has turned me into what I am.

LUCILE. (*Softly*) How horrible.

HERO. (*Coldly*) Yes. Horrible, as you say. But Tiger owes me a girl now, in exchange. And that's why I am in your bedroom tonight.

LUCILE. (*Retreating, pale*) Go away, or I'll call for help!

HERO. There's no one to call to. Besides, if that's what frightens you, set your heart at rest. I won't touch you. I only want to talk to you.
>*They look at each other, standing face to face.*
>LUCILE *cries out suddenly.*

LUCILE. I love him. I won't listen to you!

HERO. (*Sweetly*) You will, my love.

LUCILE. I'll stop up my ears!

HERO. I shall shout loud enough to make you hear. Besides, you'd soon take your hands away. No one can resist listening to their death sentence; it's too fascinating.

LUCILE. I'm not interested in your drunken, neurotic complications! I'm young and I'm sane and I love him. For a whole week I've fought with myself, all by myself I've conquered everything that kept us apart! You're wasting your time. You'll be ashamed of this ugly scene tomorrow. Go back to your own room.

HERO. Dear child, I am never ashamed . . .

LUCILE. Are you such a good friend of his wife? Besides, you know she doesn't love him! So what can it matter to you if we love each other? I'm not asking him to marry me—not even to look after me. I'll stay out of sight—I'll go on working, he can go on leading his own life, in his own world, if that's what frightens you all so much. I'm only asking you not to stop us loving each other.

HERO. (*Sneering*) His own life, his own world? What do you take me for? Papa Duval with his top hat in *La Dame aux Camélias*? It doesn't matter a damn to me.

LUCILE. Then what have you been doing ever since you came into this room? Do you think I didn't understand what was behind every word you said, even when you pretended to be fond of him and to take pity on me? Why give yourself so much trouble to try and destroy something which may be true and good, and asks nothing but the right to exist? Because you hate it?

HERO. Not even that.

LUCILE. Then why?

HERO. (*In a murmur*) I like to break things.
> *She looks at him, erect and calm. He tries to meet her gaze for a long moment, then suddenly pours out a drink and swallows it at a gulp.*

LUCILE. (*Gently*) Poor Hero. Poor little monster. You don't frighten me any more. How unhappy you must be with that load on your back.

HERO. (*Shouting suddenly*) If I'm unhappy, it's my own concern. Mind your own business!

LUCILE. It is my business. You're trying to hurt me, even now. And all I can feel for you is pity.

HERO. (*Shouting, disgusted*) I forbid you to pity me! Poor miserable little nobody of a schoolmarm! Poor pious little

THE REHEARSAL

grub, with turnip juice in her veins, tiny clean hands and feet, in her tuppenny-ha'penny dress. Poor little field mouse with her principles, her high-mindedness, her thrift! You're what I hate most in the world. What I find most stupid, most fatuous! I'd rather have a whore with an enticing belly; a tart who makes you pay every time and betrays you just the same. I'd rather have a vice-ridden hag who stuffs cocaine up her nose, a drunken tramp wallowing in her own filth under a bridge. I loathe you! And I forbid you to look at me like that.

> *He hastily pours out another glass and swallows it at a gulp. He goes up to her, barely concealing his malicious joy.*

Do you really want to know where Tiger is tonight? Do you know what was in the telegram that called him away so abruptly? Do you know what message he gave me for you?

LUCILE. (*Retreating, and crying out*) It isn't true!

HERO. What isn't true? I haven't said anything yet. (*He looks at her slyly*) Not even brave, either. I expect you cry out like that when you go to the dentist. I can just see you, even before he's reached for the drill. She looks down her nose at you, she thinks she's Joan of Arc, Antigone, and the rest of them—all the heroines in her dear little schoolbooks; then when the moment arrives, out comes the little handkerchief, the little sobs, the little tears, she's no better than anybody else. She doesn't even know how to control herself. And she has the impudence to judge you, she dares to pity you!

LUCILE. You're a monster!

HERO. What did I tell you? You try to be tactful. You observe the conventions. You put yourself out to win her confidence before you strike the final blow. You choke yourself telling her she's charming, she's desirable, and you're quite ready to console her—you or the valet. And that's all the thanks you get! (*He cries suddenly*) Come along, have hysterics—get them over quickly. I shan't go on till you've finished.

LUCILE. (*Stiffening*) I'm not going to cry.

HERO. Good. She's scornful. I prefer that. I have a horror of tears. They make me sick.
He goes toward her.
You're really beautiful at this moment. All strung up and quivering. A small animal cornered by the hounds, at bay, back to the wall. One would have to be as stupid as those two female parrots not to agree. The little poisoner of the house, the little intruder who must be shown the door. The little skeleton at the feast!

LUCILE. (*Crying out*) Say what you have to say!

HERO. (*Smiling*) You realize he's already rather late? We have plenty of time. . . . We're alone on this floor. The butler and the cook are getting drunk in the pantry and I've packed the paratrooper off to do the same in the next village. All the others are shut up in their rooms, miles away in the other wing, wondering what's going to happen next. I can see them tossing on their beds. Monsieur Damiens, hairy and dark as a fat crow who's lost his piece of cheese; Hortensia and the Countess in their silks and satins, with detective stories and sleeping pills within reach. But sleep stays away! What about the little plotter in her attic in the west wing, cooking up God knows what against the family concord and the approved liaisons . . . Won't someone manage to get rid of her at last?

He takes a step.

My dear, Tiger has suddenly realized, too late, that he has made a great mistake, the sort of mistake only he can make. If he had asked my advice beforehand, I would have told him to spare you this unhappiness. You were a virgin, virginity was your meager capital—he should never have touched it. Besides, there's something about you. I would have said to him, you can do as you please with a chambermaid, that goes without saying; if you don't have her, the footman will, either today or the day after. You're worth more than that, I admit it. But don't be too angry with him, all the same. He isn't wicked. He's a sentimentalist, an incurable sentimentalist, and it goes to his head—that's all. Besides he has every excuse. . . . It's so adorable, a new little being nestling in your arms, saying she loves you, that she belongs to you forever. Forever—for you that meant tonight—the here and now. It was a brand-new pleasure for him, something he'd never known before. He'd have had to be very high-minded to tear his arms away, to say no! And besides, as you've just told me, it's a risk all girls have to run. After all, if they ask for it. . . . The trouble is that next morning, you find the little one still loves you. "Forever," so far as she's concerned, begins with breakfast. And now you have to start worrying about her. She's deep in confidences already. The little darling, head on your shoulder, has already started to prattle about her old mother, who's so lonely, to whom one must be so very kind—of the little dishes she cooks so nicely, the name she's going to give her first baby. It's all gone, the unique joy of the night before, your sacrificial fawn. Hey presto! You're carrying the slop pail for the entire family! You can see yourself, already, pushing the pram. . . . A free translation, of course. I know that you were sensible and discreet. I'll go on working just the same; he'll never buy me anything; we shall be free; nothing will matter but our love. . . . Shall I tell you the whole truth, my dear? Yes. You're strong enough to bear it now. That's what frightened Tiger. He would rather you'd asked him for a fur coat and a nicely furnished little flat. To have a nice little mistress, in a life like his, that fits in very nicely. A great unselfish love—that is beyond price. And because he feels obscurely that he still hankers after you, that in a little while it might be even harder for him—he has come to the conclusion (put yourself in his place) that it would be better to understand each other, and use the knife right away. . . .

LUCILE. Why didn't he tell me himself?

HERO. Why should you make a hero out of that likable playboy? He knows, like all of us, ever since Napoleon gave us the tip, that there's only one cure for love—flight. He has flown. He didn't feel strong enough to let himself be caught up again. You know, dear heart, you've endowed our charming trifler with so many imaginary qualities . . .

LUCILE. (*Still stammering*) Then why did he tell me he loved me?

HERO. Emotion—fascination—contagion. Love is as catching as influenza. A certain natural eloquence, too. . . . You are young. You'll find other men. Beware of the sentimentalists, my fawn, they're the worst.

LUCILE. (*After a pause, still stiffly*) Is that all he asked you to say to me?

HERO. No, of course not. He's a gentleman. First of all, a check . . .

> *He has put his hand in his pocket. He stops as* LUCILE *recoils.*

Which you refuse, of course. I'm with you, there; I think it's clumsy. I shouldn't even have mentioned it, but after all, I'm only a messenger. Then, as I told you just now, he said: "Talk to her a little. You might try to comfort her. . . ."

> LUCILE *resists a moment, restraining herself, then suddenly falls sobbing on the bed.* HERO *goes to her.*

There. My little cardboard heroine. Let yourself go. . . . It's better to cry. . . .

> *He sits on the edge of the bed and talks to her gently, almost like a mother.*

She draws herself up, plays the proud beauty, wants to behave like a real lady and take on responsibilities. Yesterday, she was still playing with her dolls, and at the first little disappointment, she ran away to hide in her mamma's skirts. Only now—no mamma any more. She's grown-up, she's all alone. She has no one but the horrid godfather, the dry-as-dust lawyer, who has put on grandmother's pretty bonnet over his ugly wolf's head—all the better to eat you with, my dear. . . . Ah, how lonely it can be, can't it, my kitten? I know all about that. . . . You, who were a little sorry for me not so long ago, now do you understand?

> *He picks up his glass from the night table without getting up.*

There. Now she's going to have a drink. Like a good little girl.

> *He makes her drink, supporting her head.*

Then she'll have another, and another. She will have understood, yes, she will. . . .

> *He holds her against his shoulder. He isn't acting, he is crying and he murmurs:*

Evangéline . . .

> *Pause. He holds* LUCILE *to him, stroking her gently. He murmurs, looking away into the distance:*

My darling, my poor darling. Life is ugly, isn't it? She was raring to go—believed in everything, and suddenly there she was with life yawning like an abyss in front of her. She didn't say a word—she hid away so she could cry in peace, and then she married an ugly old banker the family had found for her. A beast in her bed at night, and all day the drudgery of walking up and down for his pleasure, covered in jewels. So she cries in secret for two or three years, very quietly, and then one fine day, when she's too tired, she dies—that's all, without a word, without leaving any more trace of her passing than the flight of a bird through the air.

> *He is crying. He caresses her. She is lying against his shoulder. He murmurs, his face bathed in tears:*

My child. My darling child. My poor little lost child.

> *Now he is holding her in his arms. She lets herself go.*

CURTAIN

SCENE TWO

> *The salon. Morning.* VILLEBOSSE, *alone, is in costume, furious, with his mind made up, we do not yet know to what. The* COUNT *enters, pulling on the jacket of his stage costume.*

COUNT. Here already, Villebosse? I'm late—I got home in the small hours. Forgive me for imposing a morning rehearsal on you all, but the performance is the day after tomorrow and this afternoon I shall be saddled with the orchestra. I must settle the music.

VILLEBOSSE. Sir, I've been waiting for you for an hour. It was impossible for me to speak to you alone yesterday, and I must have a serious talk with you. You seem very cheerful, sir, very happy!

COUNT. Most cheerful, Villebosse, and most happy. As I have never been before.

VILLEBOSSE. You have all the luck. Other people have none, sir. Other people suffer. Other people haven't the same reasons for rejoicing as you have, sir.

COUNT. I should hope not. For once in a while, my motives are extremely personal. Until this moment, I've been weak enough to take my pleasures in company. Now it dawns on me that happiness is a solitary exercise.

VILLEBOSSE. Is there some double meaning behind your words, sir?

COUNT. Since the invention of language, Villebosse, there has always been some double meaning behind the spoken word. In fact, words were invented expressly for that reason.

VILLEBOSSE. If there were a double meaning, sir, it would be out of place. The situation in which we find ourselves is very delicate—that should never be forgotten.

COUNT. My dear boy, it's never cost me a wink of sleep. Still, you've chosen a bad moment to bring it up, because I have decided to forget it completely.

VILLEBOSSE. What do you mean by that, sir?

COUNT. I find you a most remarkable young man, and I am charmed to have you for my wife's lover.

VILLEBOSSE. Sir, I forbid you to trifle with the lady's honor! Withdraw that word, sir, withdraw it! Or you shall give me satisfaction.

COUNT. What word?

VILLEBOSSE. The word you have just pronounced, sir. Your cynicism is a detestable pose. I will not permit it to smirch a being who has the right to our respect! The Countess, sir, is above all suspicion!

COUNT. But devil take it, Villebosse, what suspicion?

VILLEBOSSE. Sir, you understood me perfectly. Don't try to make me repeat an expression I find offensive. If you consider yourself authorized to bellow out right and left that your wife is having a love affair, you'll have to answer to me, sir.

COUNT. Villebosse, you're adorable! I never tire of listening to you and watching you evolve. You are the funniest man I've ever known.

VILLEBOSSE. *(Abashed)* I am suffering, sir, nothing more. I am sincere by nature.

COUNT. So I see.

VILLEBOSSE. No matter what I do, I shall never get used to the corruption of the degenerate little world in which you live. I come from Carcassonne, where we are simple squires. My family home has kept its moat and drawbridge since the thirteenth century. We've never budged from there, we've never put in central heating, and we've never made jokes about the honor of our wives. Withdraw that word, sir! When I knew I loved the Countess, I came and suggested to you that we should fight to the death. It was quite simple. Either I would marry the widow, or disappear. You refused.

COUNT. I wasn't ready to die that morning. Nor to kill you either. I like you very much, Villebosse.

VILLEBOSSE. You wanted it, this complex and degrading state of things!

COUNT. I wanted to live. That's always complex and degrading.

VILLEBOSSE. It can't be altered now. The honor and happiness of the Countess concern me personally. Here, then, is what I have to tell you: Sir, I will not allow you to be unfaithful to your wife!

COUNT. What!

VILLEBOSSE. You understood me perfectly. I will not tolerate your making her ridiculous, as you are doing, for the sake of a nobody. You will behave yourself, sir, from now on. Either you will behave yourself or answer for it to me.

COUNT. What are your demands, Villebosse?

VILLEBOSSE. You must break with this young person immediately. Return to the conjugal hearth. The Countess agrees to wipe the slate clean, she will forget and forgive.

COUNT. Must I break with Hortensia too?

VILLEBOSSE. She puts up with her. It's one of her weaknesses. She has always indulged you in a manner I fail to understand. Just be discreet, show the Countess more attention at all times than you do the other lady; give her precedence always. Devil take it! It's strange that it should be my business to remind you—she is your wife, sir!

COUNT. Villebosse, I love you more and more! Let me embrace you!

VILLEBOSSE. No!

COUNT. Why not? I'm sure you're very fond of me, too.

VILLEBOSSE. It would be most irregular. Keep your distance, sir! Our situation is too delicate. But never forget, I've got my eye on you!

COUNTESS. (*Entering*) When I think, Tiger, that you've succeeded in getting us all up at ten o'clock . . . But I declare, the dawn is ravishing! . . . We really should get up earlier. What a glorious morning! Did you have a good night?

COUNT. Yes, Eliane. May I have a word with you?

COUNTESS. Villebosse?

VILLEBOSSE. (*Hastening to her side*) Dearest Eliane?

COUNTESS. Would you like to make yourself useful?

VILLEBOSSE. *(Drunk with devotion)* Always!

COUNTESS. Run around all the rooms and pull out the slackers. We start rehearsing in ten minutes' time.

VILLEBOSSE. Leave it to me, Eliane, in ten minutes everyone will be here!

    When he has gone, the COUNTESS *turns toward the* COUNT.

COUNTESS. I'm listening.

COUNT. I'll try to be brief. But you're a clever woman, Eliane, and I know you'll understand.

COUNTESS. What a portentous beginning!

COUNT. Yes. I am in love with that girl.

COUNTESS. Very well.

COUNT. We've had an intelligent life together, Eliane. We've shared a mutual horror of melodrama, not because it frightens us, but because it seems to us in bad taste. You've turned a blind eye to my mistresses, and I have never asked whom you invite to tea. We have given some superb parties, our house is one of the few people really enjoy visiting and, considering what most ordinary marriages are like, ours—to put the thing in a nutshell—has been delightful.

COUNTESS. Thank you, Tiger.

COUNT. No. It's for me to thank you. I was an impossible young man, far too spoiled. We owe our success to your marvelous understanding of life. In a vociferous world, where sex is on public show and hearts grow heavier and heavier, we have kept our inward gaiety. We have lived like dancers, gracefully, matching our steps to music.

COUNTESS. (*Looking away*) And none of that attracts you any more?

COUNT. It will always seem to me the only intelligent way to live. The only way of escaping muddle and vulgarity. Only . . . (*He stops*)

COUNTESS. Only what?

COUNT. That line of my life, so graceful and so well-defined, running from my first successful ball to my probable Presidency of the Jockey Club in twenty years' time, and to my funeral at the Madeleine with all my friends in top hats . . . I am beginning to realize that though it would doubtless be a pretty memory for others, a delightful theme for an article in the *Figaro* . . . it meant nothing to me. I did not know why I was so gay all the time: I was bored.

COUNTESS. And it's that child, up in her attic, who has made you understand?

COUNT. Yes. You have too much taste, I know, Eliane, not to spare me a description of my feelings. I love her. I never knew exactly what that meant. It's stupid, it has no verve; it's graceless, it's unfunny; it has none of those qualities I thought I prized so much—but it's love.

COUNTESS. Is it so new, Tiger? I have seen you on the verge of suicide two or three times, when girls have resisted you.

COUNT. I couldn't bear to have my desires thwarted. Everything I wanted badly enough, I have to have at once. There are certain small boys who kill themselves when they're refused a bicycle. It's never very interesting. This time, I'm not even in that kind of hurry. My greatest joy is to be with her;

nothing else amuses me—but if, for one reason or another you ask me to wait, Eliane, I could wait—for a long time; without growing tired.

COUNTESS. I won't take you at your word. It would be too sad if you tried it, and lost this fine new confidence. You know I've never stopped you taking your pleasure.

COUNT. My poor Eliane, we're no longer speaking the same language. That's what frightens me. This time, there's no question of taking.

COUNTESS. I see. Then what is in question?

COUNT. *(Gently)* Giving.

COUNTESS. You've got time, you've money in your pocket. Give, my dear boy, give! What's stopping you? Take a little trip with her, buy her some new frocks. You've been saying for ten years that you wanted to go to Japan. Go to Venice and hide your amours there—I'll tell our friends you've gone to Japan.

COUNT. My poor Eliane, I'm going much farther away than Tokyo.

COUNTESS. That's the second time you've used a word I abominate. I am not your poor Eliane. Still, I really find all this very amusing, when all's said and done. Do you want us to separate, Tiger, so you can marry her?

COUNT. Why should we upset your uncle the Bishop with a divorce—have a civil servant meddling with our affairs again? It seems quite unnecessary.

COUNTESS. She hasn't asked you yet? She will within a week. These little persons, who give themselves to the first comers in their attics, have a passion for respectability.

COUNT. That is the only separation I fear, Eliane. That in your anger and spite you may use the wrong word. I have always esteemed and admired you. There is already an emerald between us. Let's not add anything else.

COUNTESS. Let me get this quite clear. We give the entertainment arranged, and the next day you leave me for as long as you love that child, for as long as she loves you? Very well, I agree. And, as you see, I'm not too worried. Enjoy yourself, Tiger, you can tell me all about it when you return.

> VILLEBOSSE *enters with* HORTENSIA. HERO *enters absently holding a glass. The* COUNTESS *suddenly goes to* HORTENSIA *and kisses her.*

COUNTESS. Dear little Hortensia! So good, so tender, so trustful! Ah! Men are worthless creatures. I'm so devoted to your scent. Hero, my little Hero, you look very depressed.... Hero, you're being unreasonable again. Hero, put down that glass—it's too early to drink.

HERO. No.
> *He sits down apart.*

VILLEBOSSE. *(To the* COUNTESS*)* He's abominably drunk, he can't even talk clearly. I defy you to rehearse with him. As for the girl and Damiens, they aren't in their rooms.

COUNTESS. Tiger, you're the only one who can find them. Will you go up, please, and bring them down?

> MONSIEUR DAMIENS *enters in street clothes, black and strange, appearing suddenly in their midst.*

M. DAMIENS. I beg you to forgive me, Madame la Comtesse. But most regretfully, I shall have to resign my part and leave the château.

COUNTESS. What are you saying, Monsieur Damiens? We're giving the performance the day after tomorrow!

M. DAMIENS. My goddaughter left for the station very early this morning, on foot and alone. This impulsive action can only be a consequence of yesterday's unhappy contretemps. After so painful an incident, I could not think of staying either.

COUNT. (*Quite pale, goes up to him*) How do you know she's gone? Perhaps she's in the village?

M. DAMIENS. When I went to her room to fetch her just now, I found this note for you on her table, Monsieur le Comte. And there was another for me.

COUNTESS. (*As the* COUNT *opens the letter*) Oh, come now, Damiens, you're dreaming! We had a very friendly chat together last night, the matter was entirely closed.

COUNT. (*Who is turned to stone, letter in hand, murmurs as in a dream*) "You were right. It was impossible. I am going away. I shall never see you again."

A silence has fallen on everyone. HERO *asks:*

HERO. Is that all?

They look at the COUNT, *who does not answer, gazing into the distance, pale as death.*

COUNTESS. It's quite extraordinary! Damiens, you who knew her . . .

M. DAMIENS. Forgive me, madame, my train leaves in a few minutes, I have only just time to get to the station. Her letter tells me nothing more, apart from her determination never to see me again either. There's no doubt she was deeply hurt, far more seriously than we thought. Now she's gone, God alone knows where, all alone and heartbroken, without shelter, without money—nothing!

COUNTESS. Good heavens! We never gave her her six months' wages!

> *The* COUNT, *who has stood silent, motionless, as if struck by lightning, suddenly rushes out.*

HORTENSIA. *(Crying out)* Tiger, where are you going?

COUNTESS. To get his car and search the roads. But which roads? Run after him, Damiens, he can drop you at the station.

M. DAMIENS. *(Going out quickly)* Goodbye, madame.

COUNTESS. *(To* HORTENSIA, *when he has gone)* The child must have taken the five o'clock but for Alençon. She'll have caught her connection there already. Tiger will never know which way she's gone. He has no hope whatsoever of finding her.

HORTENSIA. She may change her mind—write to him.

COUNTESS. Don't you believe it. Now we're free to say it, she had got a certain integrity. Her very departure proves it. She loved him—of course she did. That's why we need have no fear. After what has happened, she'll never try to see him again.

HORTENSIA. *(Suddenly gentle)* But what will Tiger do?

COUNTESS. *(Looks at her, genuinely astonished)* What a kind soul you are, Hortensia, kind to a fault! He'll be miserable for a month or two and then he'll start enjoying himself again. Besides, I know him. He has the strongest sense of his social obligations. Our first guests will be here this evening. For two days, no matter how wretched he is, he'll be unable to think of anything but his entertainment. Come, my dear, let's have some breakfast. All this has given me quite an appetite.

She begins to carry her off.

HORTENSIA. What about the part?

COUNTESS. I had foreseen the contingency. Tiger gave the part to Léonor in the first place, and she's word-perfect still. She's prepared to forget the unkind trick he played on her. She's taken the plane for Le Mans and I've sent the Renault to meet her. She'll be here in an hour. And I'll ring up Gontaut-Biron. He must be over his flu by this time.

HORTENSIA. What? You've sent for Léonor? After what you told me about her and Tiger?

COUNTESS. My dear girl, I'm very fond of you, but I'm afraid, when all's said and done, you don't fully grasp the situation. After all, our first care must be to comfort Tiger. Either I don't know him at all, or within a week he'll be thinking of nothing but Léonor. It stirs him to frenzy when people resist him. Come along and have some coffee. We both need it.

They have gone. VILLEBOSSE *runs after them, calling.*

VILLEBOSSE. Eliane, I've had no breakfast, either!

HERO. (*Still abstractedly, glass in hand, calls him back in a thick voice*) Sir!

VILLEBOSSE. (*Checking*) Sir?

HERO. One moment, if you please.

VILLEBOSSE *turns, surprised.*

I believe you're an excellent shot, sir?

VILLEBOSSE. What do you mean by that, sir?

HERO. I would even go so far as to say I believe you've won several international pistol championships?

VILLEBOSSE. That is correct.

HERO. Well, sir, I have the honor to tell you you are not loved as you would like to believe.

VILLEBOSSE. What, sir.

HERO. One is never loved as one would like to believe, that is a universal truth. But for you, there is a more particular truth. Since yesterday evening, you have been, sir—to use a word that revolts me—a cuckold.

VILLEBOSSE. *(Jumping)* You're drunk, sir! Withdraw the word!

HERO. I am drunk. But when I'm drunk I have all my wits about me. I repeat the word. It is exact. I was not in my own room last night. I was elsewhere. You understand me?

VILLEBOSSE. *(Advancing on him, terrible)* What? Do you realize what you are daring to insinuate, sir?

HERO. It seems obvious to me. Don't make me repeat an indelicate word.

VILLEBOSSE. Very well, sir. You have at least the merit of frankness. I've suspected for some time that you were trying to pick a quarrel with me. . . . We will fight. Just give me time to change my clothes.

HERO. *(Still seated)* Please hurry. I wish it to be now. I shall be waiting on the terrace.

VILLEBOSSE. At your service, sir. I'm as much in a hurry as you are.

He starts to go. HERO *calls him back.*

HERO. Sir!

VILLEBOSSE. Sir?

HERO. To regularize the position, strike me.

VILLEBOSSE. Sir, it isn't necessary.

HERO. Sir, it is. If you don't slap my face, I won't fight.

VILLEBOSSE. But we've already agreed to meet, sir. . . . I give you the choice of arms, if that's what's worrying you.

HERO. It's my privilege only if you strike me. I know the rules. Strike me at once, sir! (*He cries out, rising*) At once, dear God, or I'll throw my glass in your face! Come on, I want you to! And hard! I want to feel it. Come on, come on—you dirty cuckold! I tell you, you must!

VILLEBOSSE. Well, if you insist—you preposterous creature!
    He slaps HERO's *face.*
It's too absurd!

HERO. (*Pale, motionless, erect*) No. It's quite correct.
    He lifts a finger.
I choose pistols.

    VILLEBOSSE *bows, stiff and a little surprised at the choice, and goes out.*

    HERO *is left alone, motionless, lost in a dream. Slowly he empties his glass and lowers it from his mouth.*
Evangéline!

CURTAIN